The Foster Care System

LIVING WITH A SPECIAL NEED

The Foster Care System

JOYCE LIBAL

MASON CREST

Mason Crest
450 Parkway Drive, Suite D
Broomall, PA 19008
www.masoncrest.com

Printed in the United States of America.

Series ISBN: 978-1-4222-3027-5
ISBN: 978-1-4222-3035-0
ebook ISBN: 978-1-4222-8820-7

Library of Congress Cataloging-in-Publication Data

Libal, Joyce.
  The foster care system / Joyce Libal.
      pages cm. — (Living with a special need)
  Includes index.
  Audience: Age 12+
  Audience: Grade 7 to 8.
    ISBN 978-1-4222-3035-0 (hardback) — ISBN 978-1-4222-3027-5 (series) — ISBN
978-1-4222-8820-7 (ebook) 1. Foster home care—Juvenile literature. 2. Foster chil-
dren—Juvenile literature. 3. Child welfare—Juvenile literature. 4. Family services--Juve-
nile literature. 5. Child abuse—Juvenile literature. I. Title.
  HV873.L53 2015
  362.73'3—dc23
                                    2014010649

Picture credits: Benjamin Stewart: pp. 66, 68; Corbis: pp. 85, 88, 91; Corel: pp. 16,
107; Photo Alto: pp. 72, 104; PhotoDisc: pp. 17, 39, 40, 41, 42, 44, 50, 54, 65, 70, 73,
83, 84, 86, 97, 98, 116, 117, 118; Stockbyte: pp. 52, 53, 64, 105; Susquehanna Service
Dogs: p. 43. Individuals in these images are models, and the images are intended for illus-
trative purposes only.

CONTENTS

KEY ICONS TO LOOK FOR:

Text-Dependent Questions: These questions send the reader back to the text for more careful attention to the evidence presented there.

Words to Understand: These words with their easy-to-understand definitions will increase the reader's understanding of the text, while building vocabulary skills.

Series Glossary of Key Terms: This back-of-the book glossary contains terminology used throughout this series. Words found here increase the reader's ability to read and comprehend higher-level books and articles in this field.

Research Projects: Readers are pointed toward areas of further inquiry connected to each chapter. Suggestions are provided for projects that encourage deeper research and analysis.

Sidebars: This boxed material within the main text allows readers to build knowledge, gain insights, explore possibilities, and broaden their perspectives by weaving together additional information to provide realistic and holistic perspectives.

A child with special needs is not defined by his disability. It is just one part of who he is.

INTRODUCTION

Each child is unique and wonderful. And some children have differences we call special needs. Special needs can mean many things. Sometimes children will learn differently, or hear with an aid, or read with Braille. A young person may have a hard time communicating or paying attention. A child can be born with a special need, or acquire it by an accident or through a health condition. Sometimes a child will be developing in a typical manner and then become delayed in that development. But whatever problems a child may have with her learning, emotions, behavior, or physical body, she is always a person first. She is not defined by her disability; instead, the disability is just one part of who she is.

Inclusion means that young people with and without special needs are together in the same settings. They learn together in school; they play together in their communities; they all have the same opportunities to belong. Children learn so much from each other. A child with a hearing impairment, for example, can teach another child a new way to communicate using sign language. Someone else who has a physical disability affecting his legs can show his friends how to play wheelchair basketball. Children with and without special needs can teach each other how to appreciate and celebrate their differences. They can also help each other discover how people are more alike than they are different. Understanding and appreciating how we all have similar needs helps us learn empathy and sensitivity.

In this series, you will read about young people with special needs from the unique perspectives of children and adolescents who are experiencing the disability firsthand. Of course, not all children with a particular disability are the same as the characters in the stories. But the stories demonstrate at an emotional level how a special need impacts a child, his family, and his friends. The factual material in each chapter will expand your horizons by adding to your knowledge about a particular disability. The series as a whole will help you understand differences better and appreciate how they make us all stronger and better.

—*Cindy Croft*
Educational Consultant

YOUTH WITH SPECIAL NEEDS provides a unique forum for demystifying a wide variety of childhood medical and developmental disabilities. Written to captivate an adolescent audience, the books bring to life the challenges and triumphs experienced by children with common chronic conditions such as hearing loss, mental retardation, physical differences, and speech difficulties. The topics are addressed frankly through a blend of fiction and fact. Students and teachers alike can move beyond the information provided by accessing the resources offered at the end of each text.

This series is particularly important today as the number of children with special needs is on the rise. Over the last two decades, advances in pediatric medical techniques have allowed children who have chronic illnesses and disabilities to live longer, more functional lives. As a result, these children represent an increasingly visible part of North American population in all aspects of daily life. Students are exposed to peers with special needs in their classrooms, through extracurricular activities, and in the community. Often, young people have misperceptions and unanswered questions about a child's disabilities—and more important, his or her *abilities*. Many times, there is no vehicle for talking about these complex issues in a comfortable manner.

This series provides basic information that will leave readers with a deeper understanding of each condition, along with an awareness of some of the associated emotional impacts on affected children, their families, and their peers. It will also encourage further conversation about these issues. Most important, the series promotes a greater comfort for its readers as they live, play, and work side by side with these individuals who have medical and developmental differences—youth with special needs.

—Dr. Lisa Albers, Dr. Carolyn Bridgemohan, Dr. Laurie Glader
Medical Consultants

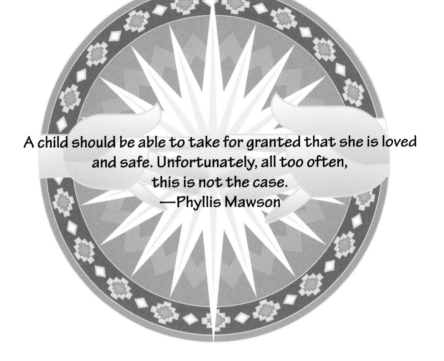

A child should be able to take for granted that she is loved and safe. Unfortunately, all too often, this is not the case.
—Phyllis Mawson

Words to Understand

indentured: Bound to work for another person for a specified period of time in order to pay off a debt.

almshouses: Poorhouses; homes for the poor.

sectarian: Parochial; having to do with a religion.

emigration: The act of leaving one's place of residence to move to another.

subsidies: Money paid by the government.

subsistence: The minimum needed to sustain life.

1

CRADLED BY UNCERTAINTY

The wire was pressed so tightly against Bobby's face that it made an imprint of the fence around his eyes and nose. Red marks faded to normal skin tones as Bobby stepped back and thought about his next move. After a moment, he dropped to the ground. Gravel scrapped against his belly as he pushed his thin arm under the chain-link divider that separated his yard and the abandoned building next door. Stretching his arm and extending his fingers, he could just touch the tiny ball of white fur. The kitten turned its wobbly head in Bobby's direction, and Bobby smiled. The kitten came a couple of shaky steps closer, and Bobby was able to relax his outstretched arm a bit as a tiny pink tongue licked his fingertip.

Glancing up, he saw the gray mother tiger cat emerge from the broken basement window. Stepping softly over shards of broken glass, she moved silently. Ever so gently, she placed the black and white bundle she had been carrying in her lips on a clump of dandelions. The black and white kitten gave a squeak of protest when she abandoned him to retrieve his sibling. Another kitten wiggled as the mother cat placed the kitten beside her brother, out of Bobby's reach.

Bobby sat up and once again pressed his face against the fence as he watched the mother cat disappear and reappear twice more. A black kitten and a tiny replica of the mother completed the family. The mother corralled her babies next to her body, and they snuggled against her for food, warmth, and security. Bobby watched, fascinated, while in the back of his mind he worried about his sister Cara.

He recognized Cara's voice crying somewhere in the distance, and sunshine and kittens faded from view as Bobby squeezed his eyes shut and tried to squeeze his ears shut too. Bobby didn't want to know why Cara was making those sounds.

His stomach rumbled as he opened his eyes and blinked. More than an hour had passed since the kindergarten bus had dropped him off at his doorstep, but Bobby didn't know that. He just knew that he was hungry. With a sigh, he got to his feet, crossed the yard, and climbed the steps to his family's apartment.

When he reached the top of the stairs, he heard a thump behind the door that held so many secrets behind it. Hungry and fearful, his hand trembled as he reached for the doorknob. Slowly and quietly he turned it, opened the door a crack, and peered inside. The television was on in Momma's bedroom, and Bobby recognized the voices of characters on her favorite soap opera. Confident that she would be in there enjoying their company, Bobby tiptoed across the living room. Approaching the kitchen door, he was gripped by fear. His three-year-old sister lay face down and motionless on the floor.

Bobby rushed to Cara's side, placed a hand against her cheek, and whispered her name. "Cara, are you okay?"

At the sound of her brother's voice, Cara lifted her face. "Bobby, I'm hungry." Tears mixed with the blood coming from her nose and red-brown stains dripped onto her favorite outfit—a pink dress, a sure sign that Cara had dressed herself that morning. Bobby grabbed the dishcloth and helped Cara wash her face and hands. Then he stepped onto the chair that Cara had fallen from and retrieved the peanut butter she was trying to reach.

The peanut butter and jelly sandwiches Bobby made tasted good, but the milk he poured into two small glasses was beginning to sour. Nevertheless, the children drank it and ate quietly as was their custom, so as not to disturb their mother. Cara loved eating lunch with her brother who always shared tales of school and bus-riding adventures. Today, her eyes grew wide as Bobby whispered about the kittens that lived next door.

"I want to see the kittens. Show me the kittens, please," she pleaded.

"Okay, but be very quiet," Bobby cautioned.

They quickly finished eating their sandwiches. Bobby held Cara's hand as they crossed the living room. They were intent on their mission, both sets of eyes focused on the door, when Cara's hand was suddenly ripped from Bobby's grip. He turned just in time to see Cara's little body hit the sofa with a thud as Momma released her. Cara uttered a surprised shriek but then fell silent. Bobby's mouth hung open in shock, and Momma slapped his chin up to shut it.

"What do you brats think you're doing sneaking out of the house behind my back?" She reached up and locked the dead bolt that was beyond their reach. Turning on her heel, she stomped toward the kitchen.

"Your father left me in charge, and you don't do anything without my permission. Look at the mess you two made! Well, you march your butts in here and clean it up right now. I'm expecting friends tonight," she shouted and returned to her bedroom.

Oh no! Bobby thought. He didn't like Momma's friends. They were all mean, and one of them was especially bad to Cara.

"Maybe we can hide while her friends are here," he whispered to his sister. "Don't cry. I'll clean the blood off the floor."

A plan was beginning to take shape in Bobby's mind. They would try to avoid trouble by being quiet and staying out of Momma's way for the rest of the afternoon. They'd build a fort at the back of the long, narrow closet in their bedroom. Remembering that his father kept a small flashlight in a kitchen drawer, Bobby opened the drawer, took the flashlight, raced quickly to the bedroom, and hid the flashlight in the closet. When he returned to the kitchen, Bobby rinsed the glasses, plates, and knife.

They had lived in several places, but the problem with this small apartment was that there weren't many hiding spots. Bobby sometimes felt bad when he hid from what was happening to Cara, but he couldn't stop Momma from doing those things, and when he interfered or cried, he got in really big trouble. Tonight he would take Cara to the closet, and they would both be safe.

"Where is Daddy? When is he coming home?" Cara whispered as she and Bobby left the kitchen.

"He's on a ship in the Navy. I don't know when he's coming home—maybe soon."

Bobby sighed. Life was nicer when Daddy was around. Sometimes he played ball with Bobby, and Cara hardly ever got hurt when Daddy was home. Also, Momma's friends never came around when Daddy was home.

Bobby and Cara spent the rest of the afternoon in their bedroom. From the window, they could see the mother cat's yard, and they watched as she carried her babies back through the broken window.

"Where's she taking them?" Cara asked.

"Into their house." Bobbie remembered watching the mother cat feed her kittens and how she lay beside them while they played, and he knew the mother cat would keep her babies safe during the night. "Let's build a fort."

Cara was reluctant to enter the dark closet at first, but when Bobby turned on the flashlight, she followed him. "How do we build it?"

Bobby didn't want to risk angering Momma by messing up the beds, so he took two blankets down from the shelf. He unfolded one of the blankets and placed it in the farthermost corner of the closet. Next, Bobby handed stacks of clothing to Cara and showed her how to pile them in front of the blanket. The second blanket was reserved for a cover.

"There," he said. "It's ready. As soon as Momma's friends get here, we'll go inside, and we'll stay there until they leave."

Cara was worried about the friends' visit, but the idea of staying in the fort with Bobby comforted her.

Everything went according to Bobby's plan. He and Cara stayed out of Momma's way until about seven o'clock when she opened a couple cans of soup. Momma's mind was on her upcoming visitors, so the meal was uneventful. After dinner, Bobby and Cara went to their room, closed the door, and waited for about an hour. Hearing a knock at the front door, they listened hard to determine who it was. When he heard a woman's voice, Bobby relaxed a bit.

"They're laughing," he told Cara. "I think it's okay."

The children looked at Cara's picture book while they continued to wait. An hour or so later, they heard a louder knock at the front door. This time they recognized a male voice.

"Don't cry," Bobby cautioned Cara. "You're going to be okay. We'll be safe in the fort."

Settling into the closet, Bobby pulled the extra blanket over their heads and turned on the flashlight.

"We need to be really quiet," he whispered. "We might have to stay here for a long time. Let's just lie down and try to sleep."

Cara nodded in agreement, but sleep didn't come easily for either child. Bobby turned off the flashlight and the two children closed their eyes, but they were listening intently for dangerous sounds beyond the closet door. Eventually, the children dozed off, only to be awakened by the sound of heavy footsteps in the hallway outside their bedroom.

"Where are the kids?"

As soon as they heard the man's gruff voice, Cara's tiny fingernails sunk into the flesh on Bobby's arm. No one responded. The children's bodies shook as they heard the door to their bedroom open.

"Shhhh." Bobby put his hand over Cara's mouth.

Unlike human children, baby rabbits (like many other animal offspring) will be independent from their mothers within a few months.

Make Connections

 Of all the offspring of animals on the earth, human beings need the most care for the longest period of time. Many animals can walk within moments of birth, for example, and are able to run from danger within weeks. Some animals begin to eat adult foods shortly after birth. Birds born in spring have all their feathers, know how to fly perfectly, and are able to migrate thousands of miles by the end of summer. Human babies, on the other hand, learn to talk and to walk very slowly, require almost constant care for several years, and must be loved and nurtured long after that in order to achieve normal development.

WHAT IS FOSTER CARE?

The word "foster" means to nurture or encourage. When a child's biological parents are unable or unwilling to properly care for their children by providing them with food, shelter, and safety, others must do so. People who are not the biological or adoptive parents of the children that they care for are providing foster care. They provide food, shelter, and safety for these children in a nurturing and encouraging environment.

Most children enter foster care because of parental abuse or chronic neglect. More than a half million children are in foster care in the United States. The majority of children who need to be placed in foster care are eventually returned to their biological families.

A PARTIAL HISTORY OF FOSTER CARE
BEFORE THE TWENTIETH CENTURY

2000 BCE	Protecting orphans was part of the code in Babylonia.
787 CE	An asylum was established for abandoned infants in Milan, Italy.
1300	The Great Code (the first document to define adoption) was written by Alphonso V of Castille. Children could only be adopted between the ages of seven and fifteen and only with permission of the king.
1500s–1600s	Laws in England and North America allowed orphans and poor or abandoned children to be *indentured* to business people and others. Children often remained in this service until they turned eighteen.
1617	A number of children from Christ's Hospital, a home for orphans in London, set sail for North America as apprentices of the Virginia Company.
1636	A seven-year-old boy named Benjamin Eaton became the first foster child in the United States.
1700s–1800s	*Almshouses* were established in New York and other cities. Moral instruction and trades were sometimes taught at these publicly funded shelters for the homeless. Adults were also housed at almshouses where they were not separated from children, and many abuses took place. Adults wishing to secure children as servants or for other labor could adopt them from these shelters. After such adoptions, no one was certain that the children were

adequately cared for because no one checked on the children.

1741   The London Foundling Home was established.

1849   A minister named Charles Loring Brace established the Children's Aid Society in response to the large number of children (as many as thirty thousand) living on the streets of New York City. In 1853, he developed the Placing Out System, which used Orphan Trains (sometimes called Mercy Trains or Baby Trains) to transport children from New York City to other parts of the country. Families selected and adopted children in exchange for the labor they could provide on farms, in businesses, or around the house. This led to the involvement of individual states and **sectarian** organizations in child placement. By 1929, as many as two hundred thousand children had been adopted through the Placing Out System.

1865   Massachusetts was among the first states to reimburse families who cared for children that were too young for indentured service.

1868   Almshouses were banished in New York; instead, the establishment of orphanages was recommended. In the 1860s, laws that required children be removed from almshouses were passed in several states. Between 1868 and 1924, philanthropists and organizations in Great Britain sent as many as eighty thousand orphans and homeless children (known as British Home

Children) to Canada to be apprenticed to farmers and businesses or to become domestic servants. Most of these children were under the age of fourteen. By 1948, the number of children included in this forced *emigration* had risen to over one hundred thousand.

1869   The National Children's Home and Orphanage was established in England. Laws were passed regarding the labor and education of children.

1885   Pennsylvania began requiring a license in order to care for two or more unrelated children.

1886   Charles Britwell, a member of the Boston Children's Aid Society, established supervised foster homes where an effort was made to secure placement based on the child's needs. He also promoted the idea of reimbursing foster families for child-care expenses and eventually returning children to the care of their biological parents.

1893   The Children's Home Society began receiving *subsidies* from the state of South Dakota.

FIRST *DOCUMENTED* CASE OF CHILD ABUSE IN THE UNITED STATES

In 1874, a member of a local charity heard that a woman was abusing a ten-year-old child named Mary Ellen and went to the woman's home to investigate the charge. When she was only eighteen months old, Mary Ellen had been left with her baby-sitter. Since her mother did not return, the baby was sent to an almshouse run by the city. After six

In the 1800s, people began to consider that society might owe children help and protection.

months, she was released to the care of a foster mother. The worker discovered Mary Ellen chained to a bed. Her body had many scars and bruises.

At this time, there were no laws prohibiting child abuse, but the Society for the Prevention of Cruelty to Animals existed. So the worker asked if they would prosecute the case on Mary Ellen's behalf. Mary Ellen testified that her foster mother whipped and beat her almost every day and that she had no recollection of ever having been kissed. The foster mother was convicted and sent to prison for a year. Mary Ellen was sent to the home of another foster family.

In 1875, as a result of Mary Ellen's case, the first child protection laws were established and the New York Society for the Prevention of Cruelty to Children was formed. Other states soon began creating similar agencies to protect children.

By the nineteenth century, most Americans believed that "Uncle Sam" was responsible for children from a variety of ethnic backgrounds. The government's care, however, was seldom based on an adequate understanding of the real needs and value of the ethnic groups.

BENEFITS AND ABUSES OF THE PLACING OUT SYSTEM AND THE BRITISH HOME CHILDREN MOVEMENT

Benefits

- Many children were placed in a better situation than they endured previously while living in almshouses or other institutions or being homeless and begging for **subsistence**.
- The sparse populations of certain states and provinces were increased.
- Many children learned trades that helped to prepare them for an improved future.
- Some children were adopted into caring families.

Research Project

Find out what it was like to be a "home child" in nineteenth-century Canada. Read *Orphan at My Door: The Home Child Diary of Victoria Cope* by Jean Little.

Text-Dependent Questions

1. Describe what a foster parent does.
2. What was Charles Loring Brace's role in the history of foster care?
3. Describe what happened in the first documented case of child abuse in the United States.

Abuses

- Adults were not always properly screened prior to being allowed to adopt children.
- Children were often forced to stand on platforms and endure inspection by those wishing to adopt.
- Though some children knew which families were to receive them before they left on an orphan train, many were shipped into the unknown without any attempt to match their needs to what an individual family had to offer.
- Children often ended up being indentured servants rather than loved and respected family members.
- Some British Home Children were sold to farmers, so profit became a motive for sending children to Canada.
- Many of the children who were sent to Canada were not orphans, and some of these children were sent without parental consent or even parental knowledge.
- Many siblings were separated and never saw each other again.
- Many children suffered because of loneliness, neglect, difficult labor, discrimination, and abuse.

How can we expect children to learn in the classroom when their lives at home are ruled by fear?
—Roberta Bolles

2

COLORING OUTSIDE
THE LINES

Although the bedroom was dark, the man was apparently not deterred. His footsteps crossed the floor, coming closer to the closet door. The children held their breaths.

"Where are you going?" a female voice inquired. "Bill just got here with the good stuff."

The bedroom door closed, and both sets of footsteps faded into the distance. Bobby let out a sigh of relief as he removed his hand from Cara's mouth. Cara's sweaty body shook as she turned and clutched Bobby.

The remainder of the evening was quiet in the closet, but many hours passed before Bobby and Cara fell asleep. It was late Saturday morning when the children gathered enough courage to leave their sanctuary. Momma was still in her bedroom, and, thankfully, all her friends were gone. The children stepped gingerly around empty liquor bottles and the other debris that now littered the apartment. After eating cereal with the remainder of the souring milk, Bobby had an idea.

"Let's clean up everything before Momma wakes up—so she won't get mad when she sees it."

"Okay," Cara agreed, and the children placed the bottles and other items in a trash bag.

This pattern of life for Bobby and Cara continued for the next couple of years: stay out of Momma's way, clean up every mess, don't make any noise, and try to keep Cara as safe as possible. Things were always better when Daddy was home on leave, but that didn't happen nearly as often as Bobby and Cara wished.

Bobby had enjoyed kindergarten, but first grade was harder for several reasons. The family moved twice, and Bobby had to change schools each time. It always seemed like Bobby was in the middle of learning something important when he had to move. Then he'd enroll in a new school, and the class would be in the middle of lessons that were foreign to him. Bobby just couldn't catch up, and he felt stupid. Leaving friends behind was sad, too, and making new ones was difficult. He was relieved when first grade was over.

Now that he was about to start second grade, he hoped that they wouldn't have to move anymore. Maybe if he started the year out fresh with all the other kids, he'd understand everything and be able to keep up with his lessons.

Cara was entering kindergarten, and she had been thoroughly prepared by her brother. She remembered the exciting stories Bobby used to tell her over lunch when he first went to school, and she felt comforted by those memories. Bobby held Cara's hand as she boarded the bus for the first time. Unfamiliar faces met her gaze as she mounted the top step. She was nervous, but having Bobby at her side was reassuring. She cast her eyes meekly toward the floor, but her face held a slight smile as together they walked to an empty seat. So long as she was with Bobby, she knew she was safe.

Other less familiar feelings tugged at Cara that morning, although she didn't consider them on a conscious level. For the first time in her life, Cara was experiencing a mixture of profound relief and freedom. Bobby had told her that teachers didn't hurt children, and Cara relished the knowledge that each weekday she would be safe in school.

She saw several men and women waiting at the curb when the bus pulled up to Oakdale Elementary School.

"They're teachers' aides," Bobby explained. "They'll call us off the bus by grade and walk with us to class."

The sixth graders were asked to leave the bus first, then the fifth, and so on. Cara's courage exited the bus along with Bobby when the second graders were summoned. She was surprised to notice her thin knees shaking as she got up when the kindergarteners were finally called.

A second surprise met her as she approached her classroom. The hall was crowded with parents who had driven their kids to school. Some were telling their children that everything was going to be okay, others were taking photographs before saying good-bye, and one mother even cried when her little boy turned to enter the kindergarten classroom. Cara stepped through the doorway alone and overwhelmed.

There were several short tables with child-sized chairs, just as Bobby had predicted, but Cara didn't know where to go or what to do. She remained motionless until the teacher said hello, shook Cara's hand, and asked her name. While pinning a pretty name tag on Cara's dress, the teacher invited Cara to take a seat. Cara walked over to an empty table, sat down, neatly folded her hands together, and placed them in her lap. A girl at the next table covered her mouth with her hand and whispered to the friend sitting beside her. They looked at Cara and giggled. A little shudder rippled through Cara's body.

That incident and the unpleasant feeling associated with it would be among the things she later remembered most about her first year of school. The unfortunate cupcake fiasco was another.

On that first day of school, the mother of one of Cara's new classmates delivered cupcakes to the class. When the children returned from recess later that morning, a cupcake was waiting at each of their places. Cara hadn't had breakfast that morning, and the sweet aroma drifted up to her nose. Cara remembered watching someone make cupcakes on TV, but she had never actually eaten one before. The cupcake was still encased in its pink paper wrapper when Cara suddenly lifted it to her mouth and took a big bite. Laughter rang in Cara's ears as she lifted her frosting-covered face from the cupcake and realized that the laughter was directed at her.

"Children, you may eat your cupcakes now." The teacher handed Cara a napkin. As Cara wiped frosting from her cheeks and nose, she watched the other children take the paper wrappers off their cupcakes before biting into them.

After the cupcakes, all that was left to do before leaving school that day was to color a picture. Cara was used to drawing using a pencil or a pen, but she and Bobby had never owned coloring books. As she opened the box of crayons, the rows of beautiful, waxy hues with sharp, inviting points excited her. An elephant dancing in a tutu lay before Cara, and without thought for the normal color of elephants, she colored the picture with enthusiasm. The boy sitting next to her chuckled.

"You made your elephant green," he stated.

"So?" Cara replied.

"And you didn't stay inside the lines. Your picture is scribbled."

Cara glanced at several pictures being more neatly colored by other children at her table. When she looked back at her green elephant with color outside its lines, a tear rolled down her cheek.

Unfortunately, that first day of school set the pace for Cara's entire year. She felt different from the other children—like an outcast. Making friends seemed impossible, and she eventually gave up trying. She became an observer more than a participant in class. The good thing about school, from her point of view, was that no one hurt her physically while she was there. But for Cara, school had its own set of painful experiences.

When the end of the year rolled around, Cara discovered she was being held back in kindergarten.

"Who ever heard of someone flunking kindergarten?" her mother shouted when she heard the news. "Are you the dumbest kid on the planet?"

The force of the blow to Cara's face sent her body to the floor, and her mother's foot came down hard on Cara's arm as she stepped across her.

Many years later, Cara learned that the teacher held her back because she felt Cara was emotionally immature, but right now being held back made Cara agree with her mother: she was the stupidest kid around. The thought of having to repeat kindergarten while everyone else moved on to first grade made her squirm. She wished that her family would move to a new house so that she'd never have to see these kids again.

But kindergarten went better for Cara the second time around. Everything was familiar, she knew where to sit, she knew how to eat cupcakes, and coloring inside the lines was easy now. Cara befriended the child who looked the most frightened on the first day of school, so Cara now had a friend.

But she still felt out of place. She had grown a lot during the summer, and she was much taller than this group of younger kids. She felt like a giant.

Her most prominent memory of the second year of kindergarten turned out to be the horror caused by the head lice epidemic. Several children had already been sent home from school because of the nasty bugs when it became clear that Cara would have the same fate.

Daddy was home when the nurse made the telephone call. Cara heard her calmly explain what needed to be done, and her father stopped at the pharmacy to purchase the necessary shampoo on his way to the school. Frightened because she had head lice and fearful of what would happen next, Cara cried during the ride home while her father tried to reassure her.

"Don't worry, Cara. The shampoo kills the lice. Mommy will take care of it as soon as we get home."

That's what I'm afraid of, Cara thought. She knew her mother would not be happy that there were creatures living in Cara's hair. This was bound to cause big trouble. Momma was waiting in the bathroom when Cara and her father entered the house.

"She said to send you right up as soon as we got here." Cara's father turned her toward the stairs and gave an encouraging nudge.

"Set it down by the sink," Momma said quietly between gritted teeth as Cara held the shampoo out to her. "You dirty, disgusting little brat." Momma slammed the door.

Cara tried to be quiet as her mother demanded, but a scream soon escaped her lips and reached her father in the kitchen. The newspaper and coffee sat deserted on the table as Cara's father raced up the stairs.

"What's going on?" he shouted. He saw the steam rising through the air, and he pulled Cara's head out of the boiling-hot water. Several clumps of Cara's long, silky hair disappeared down the drain.

"What are you doing?" He grabbed Cara's mother by the arm. "Get out of here. I'll finish this."

Cara could only sob. She was used to many kinds of pain, but she had never before had her head dipped in scalding water.

"I'm sorry, Cara," her father said. "I'm sure Mommy is just upset about the lice. She didn't mean to hurt you."

Cara wanted to shout that he was wrong, but she was afraid. Momma had warned Cara many times that if Cara ever told Daddy or anyone else about the things Momma did, she would kill Bobby. Cara believed her mother was quite capable of killing her. She knew that Momma had cautioned Bobby in the same manner, threatening to him as well that she would kill Cara if he told anyone about went on in their home. The horrible secret lay buried within both children until one day the next year.

Daddy was on a ship again, and Momma had a party with some of her friends. Cara wasn't feeling well on Monday morning after the party, but staying home was the last thing she wanted, so she dressed and went to school.

The teacher looked at Cara disapprovingly as she squirmed in her seat. Cara was having difficulty in first grade. Reading was especially confusing for her, and Mrs. Halifax was always saying that Cara's mind wandered when she should be concentrating on her work.

"Cara, sit up straight." Cara heard the annoyance in Mrs. Halifax's voice.

But pain would not allow Cara to sit up straight, and she continued to change position frequently.

"Cara, what's wrong? You're disturbing other people in the class, and you can't tell me that you're concentrating on your math problems when you're wriggling around like that."

"My back hurts." Cara regretted the words the moment she spoke.

"What do you mean, your back hurts? Did you fall down?"

"No," Cara replied. "It's just bothering me."

"Well, I think you'd better take your bothering back down to the nurse's office. Here's a note. I'll call Ms. Beeler and tell her you're on your way."

Cara entered Ms. Beeler's office nervously and handed the nurse the note.

Ms. Beeler read the slip of paper and then looked up at Cara. "Does your back usually hurt—or is this a new pain? Did you fall down? Where does it feel bad?"

The questions were coming fast, and Cara couldn't think straight enough to answer them. She didn't know what to say. There was no way she could tell the truth, and she couldn't come up with a believable lie on the spur of the moment, so she just shook her head no to all the questions.

"Well, let's have a look." Ms. Beeler got to her feet and came around her desk. "I'm going to move your shirt up just a little bit, Cara, so that I can see your back."

She gently lifted Cara's blouse. Cara heard Ms. Beeler suck in her breath. "Oh Cara," she said softly.

A PARTIAL HISTORY OF FOSTER CARE
DURING THE TWENTIETH CENTURY

1900s   Social agencies began keeping more records of individual children's situations, and their specific needs were more often considered when making foster home placements. Foster parents began to come under increasing supervision by social agencies. States began inspecting foster homes, and increasing services were provided to biological families to promote reunification of families.

1909   The White House Conference on Dependent Children was held.

1912   President Theodore Roosevelt established the United States Children's Bureau, which became responsible for child welfare.

1930s   The idea of determining the suitability of foster homes and approving them for child care was promoted. Increasing numbers of foster parents were reimbursed for child-care expenses. A growing number of agencies began to match children to specific foster homes.

1932   Approximately one-third of the social welfare agencies being operated privately in the United States prior to 1929 had discontinued operations by 1932.

1935   The Social Security Act was passed during the administration of President Franklin Roosevelt. Among other things, the act called for federal money to be allocated to states to provide for various aspects of child welfare.

1950s	People began to realize that, rather than being a temporary solution, foster care was becoming permanent for many children.
1956	The Department of Health, Education, and Welfare was established by the federal government.
1959	The Child Welfare League of America conducted a study on foster care in the United States. The results of the study suggested that children were sometimes unjustly removed from biological parents. Furthermore, it found that many children were in unsatisfactory foster homes and that children who were members of minorities and children of economically depressed families were overrepresented in the foster-care system and underrepresented in adoptions. Those conducting the study also felt that not enough emphasis was being placed upon the reunification of families.
1960s	There was a continuous decline in the number of orphanages being operated and a growing number of foster families caring for children, although many children with special needs were placed in group homes rather than foster homes.
1962	Experts in the field of child welfare and reform made an effort to heighten public awareness of child abuse through publication of their findings and views in *The Battered Child*.
1964	President Lyndon Johnson declared war on poverty.

1970s	The government and child-care agencies began to question the desirability of long-term foster care.
1974	Congress passed the Child Abuse Prevention and Treatment Act, which led states to develop and enact laws mandating the report of child abuse to appropriate agencies. It also provided procedures to be followed when investigating cases of *alleged* neglect and abuse.
1976	Public knowledge of child neglect and abuse increased, more money was provided to foster families for the care of children in need, and there were over one hundred thousand children in foster care in the United States.
1980	There was a growing feeling that, as much as possible, the best situation for children in most instances was to live with their biological parents. Passage of the Adoption Assistance and Child Welfare Act allocated funds for use in programs that aimed to reduce the need for foster care by working toward prevention of family problems and toward the reunification of families.
1986–1997	The number of cases of neglected and abused children rose 114 percent.
1990	Congress passed the Victims of Child Abuse Act.
1996	Twenty-seven thousand children were adopted out of foster care.
1997	The Adoption and Safe Families Act was passed by Congress during President Bill Clinton's administration.

WHAT ARE THE MAIN FEATURES OF THE ADOPTION AND SAFE FAMILIES ACT?

- The law states that the health and safety of children are a paramount concern and requires states to make all reasonable efforts to avoid having to place children in foster care.
- When children are placed in foster care, the law requires that they eventually be returned to their biological parents unless doing so presents a danger to the children.
- Permanency plans (usually adoption but certain other options such as kinship care or guardianship also qualify) must be developed for all foster children who have not been reunited with their biological parents within one year. Even less time (six months) is allowed for parental *reunification* with children who are less than three years old.
- According to the law, reunification efforts and alternative permanency planning can be conducted *concurrently* so that less time elapses between initial foster placement and a permanent solution.
- Goals for adoption of children out of foster care were set, and monetary incentives were provided to states and counties that exceeded those goals. The allotments were four thousand dollars for each adoption over the established goal and six thousand dollars per adoption if the child was identified as having special needs.
- The law encourages states to look beyond their areas of *jurisdiction* for suitable placements for children who are waiting for adoption. There are financial penalties for delaying or denying adoptive placement of children to approved families living outside of a state's jurisdiction.

- The law created a movement toward increased adoption, and the number of children eligible for adoption increased dramatically after passage of the act. California experienced a 287 percent increase, for example. The number of families desiring to adopt did not keep pace with that acceleration, however.
- A goal was set to double the number of adoptions (from twenty-seven thousand to fifty-four thousand) by 2002. This was called the Adoption 2000 Initiative. (Information taken from the AFCARS Report, Washington, DC: Children's Bureau, U.S. Department of Health and Human Services, available online at www.acf.hhs.gov/programs/cb.)

FAMILY FOSTER CARE FACT SHEET

Children in Care

There were approximately 400,540 children in the foster care system in the United States in 2011. There are 6,000 fewer than the year before and fifty percent more than in 1987.

Age of Children in Foster Care

In 2011, the estimated average age of children in foster care was 9.3 years. The age breakdown of children in foster care is as follows:

Age Group	Percentage	Number of Children
<1 year	6.0	24,439
1 thru 5 years	32.0	127,260
6 thru 10 years	21.0	80,544
11 thru 15 years	23.0	90,879
16 thru 18 years	18.0	70,761
19 + years	2.0	6,258

A very small percentage of Asian children are in foster care.

More than half of all the children in foster care are children of color. This fact may relate to the unequal economic and educational opportunities encountered by many ethnic groups.

Race/Ethnicity

In 1980, 47 percent of children in foster care were children of color. By 2011, 59 percent of children in foster care were children of color. Children of color are disproportionately represented in the foster-care system. In 1990, for the first time, there were more African American children than white children in foster care.

Ethnicity	Percentage
Black Non-Hispanic	27%
Asian/Pacific Islander Non-Hispanic	1%
White Non-Hispanic	41%
Hispanic	21%
American Indian/Native Alaskan	2%
Unknown	7%

If a child is physically challenged or has some other disability, it may be especially hard to find him a good foster home.

Research Project

Learn more about what it's like to be a foster child by reading *The Guardian* by Joyce Sweeny. It's a novel about a thirteen-year-old boy named Hunter who has been shifted from foster home to foster home for most of his life.

Text-Dependent Questions

1. Describe what the Child Welfare League of America learned in 1959.
2. How did President Bill Clinton's administration contribute to the safety of children?
3. How does the number of children in foster care in 2011 compare to the number in 2010 and 1987?
4. What age group of children in foster care is largest?

Gender

Gender	Percentage
Male	52%
Female	48%

Permanency Plan of Children in Foster Care

Permanency Plan	Percentage	Number of Children
Reunify with parent(s) or principal caretaker(s)	52%	199,123
Live with other relatives	3%	13,420
Adoption	25%	94,629
Long-term foster care	6%	22,744
Emancipation	5%	20,635
Guardianship	4%	14,593
Case plan goal not yet established	5%	19,324

Words to Understand

Department of Social Services: Government office that provides services having to do with welfare to qualified individuals.

Child Protective Services: The division of a social service agency that investigates allegations of child abuse or neglect.

intervention: The act of entering into and affecting the affairs of others; mediation or entrance into a situation having to do with other people, such as a family.

caseworkers: People who are employed by social service agencies to work directly with assigned individuals and families.

symmetrical: Appearing the same on opposite sides of a center point or line; having two identical sides.

social workers: Individuals who have either a bachelor's degree, master's degree, or Ph.D. in social work. They perform various types of work, including assessing families applying for adoptions or administering group foster homes. Only social workers with a master's degree or Ph.D. may provide psychotherapy to socially maladjusted individuals and families.

psychologists: Individuals who have studied the science of the mind and behavior of individuals and groups and received a bachelor's degree, master's degree, or Ph.D. in psychology. They perform various types of work, including testing, conducting research, or providing counseling in this field. Only psychologists with a master's degree or Ph.D. may provide psychotherapy.

psychiatrists: Medical doctors who specialize in the diagnosis and treatment of mental and emotional disorders.

liability coverage: Insurance that covers certain types of damage.

3

THE DISCOVERY

Ms. Beeler let Cara's blouse drop back to its original position. She was silent for a second, and then she walked around so she could face Cara.

"I can see that your back hurts quite a lot," she said gently, "and we need to get some medicine for it." She patted Cara's shoulder. "I'm going to call a friend of mine who'll be able to help us. Everything is going to be fine. We're going to get your back all fixed up, and you're going to be safe. I'm going to ask Mrs. Katz to stay here with you while I call my friend, and then I'll be right back with the medicine. I don't want you to worry about anything."

After Ms. Beeler closed the office door, she telephoned Children and Youth, a branch of the county-operated **Department of Social Services**. She asked to speak with the director of the **Child Protective Services** office. Ms. Beeler had been working at the school for many years, and over that time she became acquainted with many children whose families received **intervention** services. That's how she met the director of this office and several of the **caseworkers** at the social service agency. She also knew some of the foster families who lived within the school district.

"I have a seven-year-old girl in my office," she said into the phone. "She complained of back pain in class, so the teacher sent her to see me. As it turns out, she has **symmetrical** rows of burns on each side of her spine. It looks like they were made by a cigarette."

"Poor kid. These things never fail to amaze, do they? Well,

47

luckily it's early morning. That'll give us time to get all the necessary paperwork filled out and conduct the interviews and medical exam. Have you treated the burns at all?"

"No, I wanted to call right away to be certain you'd be able to get the ball rolling. But I am going to apply some minor medication now."

"Okay, Sharon is the CPS investigator who is going to get this assignment. I'll have to fill her in, and I'm sure she'll be there shortly. Are there any siblings?"

"Yes, there's a brother in fourth grade."

"Okay, we're going to need to include him. We'll want to interview both children and talk to the school psychologist. Sharon will be there soon. Can you have Mrs. Katz fax information on the children over to my office right away?"

Ms. Beeler returned to the room where Cara waited. As the nurse lightly applied soothing salve to each burn, she could see that Cara's physical pain began to immediately subside. *If only mental anguish could be so easily extinguished*, Ms. Beeler thought.

The remainder of the day was a blur of activity that changed the course of life for both Cara and Bobby. The children were unaware of the papers being filled out, faxed, copied, and filed. They didn't realize that voices were crisscrossing the city's telephone wires between the school, social service office, hospital, police department, and courthouse on their behalf. How could they have known that a network of **social workers**, **psychologists**, **psychiatrists**, lawyers, judges, police officers, doctors, and more were in place and ready to help children like them? They would be sheltered from most of the details and activities carried on by these adults according to federal and state laws that govern child welfare.

Shortly after Bobby entered the nurse's office, Ms. Beeler introduced both Cara and Bobby to a woman named Sharon. Sharon explained that it was her job to help children by keeping them safe and that she hoped to become a very good friend to them. Within the whirlwind of activities that took place that day, they spoke to the school psychologist and a nice doctor. The scars on Cara's body provided many clues to her past, but it wasn't necessary for the doctor and psychologist to make educated guesses about everything that happened, because Bobby and Cara finally decided to tell them the truth about their mother.

The children did not return home that evening. Instead, Sharon drove them to a private residence that was licensed to offer emergency foster care. Sharon explained that Mr. and Mrs. Rodriguez were nice people who often let children stay at their house for short visits. She asked the children if they liked dogs and told them Mr. and Mrs. Rodriguez had a very friendly dog that loved to play fetch with kids. Both Bobby and Cara were excited because they had always wanted pets, but the closest they had ever come to having any was the family of stray cats they befriended when Bobby was in kindergarten. Still, Bobby and Cara were scared.

"Does Mom know where we are?" Bobby's voice quivered. "Is she coming over here?"

"No. She knows that you are in a safe place, and that kind people are going to be taking care of you." Sharon said.

"What about Dad?" Bobby asked.

"Andrea, my coworker, is still trying to reach him on his ship. We hope to be able to speak with him either tonight or tomorrow."

As Sharon pulled her car onto the cobblestone driveway at the Rodriguez's residence, Cara reached across the backseat and grabbed Bobby's hand. Fear of the unknown filled their faces as they silently looked into each other's eyes.

WHAT ARE THE REQUIREMENTS TO BECOME A FOSTER PARENT?

Foster care can be administered by government or by licensed private agencies. Requirements differ somewhat from one agency to the next, but many things are fairly common.

The Adoption and Safe Families Act requires a criminal background check in most instances. This is usually also required of prospective adoptive parents. Those who have been convicted of certain crimes cannot become foster or adoptive parents. These crimes include: felony child abuse or neglect or other crimes involving children including child pornography; rape, sexual assault, or other violent crimes,

A foster child needs to know she will be safe in her temporary home.

including murder; spousal abuse; or felony physical assault, battery, or drug-related offenses occurring within five years of application.

Other things that are usually required of foster parents include the following:

- legal age (twenty-one in some cases and eighteen in others)
- good health as proven by a medical exam
- employed or retired
- references
- own or rent a home or apartment with enough space for foster children
- willing to allow a home inspection
- able to provide a minimum time commitment
- attend training provided by the agency or others deemed appropriate by the agency
- ability to work with social service providers as part of a team
- willingness to work toward a child's reunification with biological parents
- ability to maintain confidentiality where necessary
- ability to share information when appropriate

WHAT SHOULD FOSTER PARENTS BE PREPARED TO OFFER A FOSTER CHILD?

- proper nutrition
- a safe and nurturing environment
- scheduling of and transportation to needed dental, medical, therapeutic, court, or other appointments
- needed help with schoolwork
- recreational opportunities
- patience and empathy in helping children deal with traumatic experiences and mixed emotions

- a positive parenting role model
- good communication and problem-solving skills

Some of these things can be enhanced through training provided by the social service agency.

WHAT ARE THE FIRST STEPS IN BECOMING A FOSTER PARENT?

Make a telephone call to your local social service agency, state your interest, and request information and an application.

Information and an application may be mailed to you, or you might be invited to attend an informational meeting, or

No child should have to live in the streets. If parents cannot provide adequate shelter, clothing, and food, the child may be placed in a foster home.

Make Connections: What Kind of People Become Foster Parents

All types of people become foster parents including the following:
- young or old
- married or single
- heterosexual or homosexual
- religious or nonreligious
- all economic backgrounds as long as there are sufficient funds to properly care for foster children
- all cultural backgrounds

you may be asked if you would like to make an appointment to speak with a social service worker.

WHAT TYPE OF SUPPORT IS AVAILABLE TO FOSTER PARENTS?

- Initial training and annual training provided by the social service agency. (The type of training and number of hours spent in training will depend on the children you desire to be licensed to care for and

Research Project

Here's another book to read about someone who experienced foster care: *One for the Murphys* by Lynda Mullaly Hunt. Twelve-year-old Carley Connors is placed in foster care after her mother is badly beaten and hospitalized.

Text-Dependent Questions

1. List some of the things a foster parent must be able to give to a foster child.
2. Describe the people who become foster parents.

specific requirements of the agency you are dealing with.)

- Monthly financial compensation and sometimes additional compensation for many of the expenses involved in housing and caring for foster children.
- Support from caseworkers and professional social service staff.
- Medicaid or health insurance for the foster child.
- In some cases *liability coverage* might be provided.
- Foster parent organizations or newsletters where foster parents can discuss problems and exchange information with each other may be available locally or can be accessed over the Internet.

Safety should not be a luxury for our children.
—Alexa Bierce

Words to Understand

ethnic: Having to do with race, culture, or customs.
federal subsidies: Money that is provided by the federal government.
delinquent: Having to do with behaviors that are against the law.

4

EMERGENCY SHELTER

Cara and Bobby had never been to this part of town before.
"That's the college," Sharon pointed out as they passed a cluster of ivy-covered buildings two blocks before the Rodriguez's home. Tall sycamores framed the roadway, and pretty painted fences that separated one yard from the next. To the children's eyes, Mr. and Mrs. Rodriguez's two-story red brick house look like it belonged in a fairytale; but this had been a shocking, life-changing day, and the home's inviting look did little to calm their fears.

Mr. Rodriguez heard Sharon's car moving slowly down Sycamore Avenue even before the dog began to bark in the house, alerting the couple to company. He got up slowly from the flowerbed that had held his attention for most of the afternoon. His knees ached as he pulled his body to attention and turned to greet this new set of visitors. Mr. and Mrs. Rodriguez had acted as a short-term, emergency foster-care family for many children over the past ten years, and the awkward introductions that were about to take place were already familiar.

Inside the home, Mrs. Rodriguez quickly removed her paint-stained apron when Bentley began to bark. "You stay, Bentley." She slipped past the excited dog and went outside to say hello.

The gate was open and Mr. and Mrs. Rodriguez waited in the driveway while Sharon turned off the ignition. The gray curl that fell over Mrs. Rodriguez's forehead was tipped with purple paint.

"Hello, you must be Cara and Robert," Mrs. Rodriguez said. "Let's go in the house to talk. Are either of you children afraid of dogs?"

"No," Bobby answered for both of them. "We like dogs."

Mr. and Mrs. Rodriguez both noted the eager tone in Bobby's reply and the fact that Cara was silent.

A spotted fox terrier jumped up and down as the children entered the living room. Antique chairs and a velvet couch sat before the tailored fireplace, and books bound in leather filled shelves on one wall. Bobby and Cara felt like fish out of water in the unfamiliar setting, yet they liked this room that smelled of furniture polish and leather. Bentley eagerly squeezed his body between the two sets of thin legs that dangled from the sofa, stood on his hind legs, placed his front paws upon the soft velvet, and tried to straddle both of the children's laps with his square head. Two hands reached simultaneously for the wiry fur between Bentley's ears.

The children remained silent. Mrs. Rodriguez suspected they were thirsty—children always seemed to be—but when she offered glasses of juice, Bobby answered, "No thank you," and Cara turned her head from side to side. The children were obviously listening intently as Sharon and the Rodriguezes began to discuss the situation.

"I've already explained to the children that it's our job to keep them safe and to make sure that they are well cared for," Sharon began. "I haven't spoken with their father yet, but either Andrea or I should be talking to him by tomorrow at the latest. I spoke with someone else at the Navy, and it sounds like it may be a while before Mr. Cooper can get here."

Sharon turned toward the children. "Cara and Bobby, we're going to plan on the two of you staying with Mr. and Mrs. Rodriguez for at least two weeks. I'm going to ask your father to telephone you here as soon as I speak with him, so each of you kids will be able to talk to him when he calls, okay? Do you have any questions?"

"How are we going to get to school?" Bobby asked.

"That's a good question, Bobby," Mrs. Rodriguez replied. "You've had a very busy day today, and we have a lot to do tomorrow, too, so you are going to have the day off from school. After that, I'm going to drive you and Cara to school and pick you up every day."

"Do the kids at school know what happened?" Bobby asked.

"No," Sharon answered. "Cara's classmates know that she went to the nurse's office because of her back pain, and I'm sure your class realizes that you were later called down there. That's all they know, and it's all they need to know."

"What's going to happen when Dad gets here?"

"I'm not sure of everything that's going to happen yet," Sharon answered. "He and I need to discuss that. I feel certain he'll want to visit both of you as soon as he can."

"What about Momma?" Cara asked quietly.

"Well," Sharon began, "your mother is fine, but people are talking to her right now. It will be a while before I have more information for you about your mother." She smiled at the two children. "If there aren't any more questions, I'm going to call it a day and let the four of you begin settling in. I have the kids' school books out in the car."

"I'll walk you out and collect the kids' books," Mr. Rodriguez offered.

"And I'll start showing Bobby and Cara around the house, starting with the downstairs. Is Bobby the name that you prefer to be called?" Mrs. Rodriguez asked.

Bobby nodded.

Mr. Rodriguez had a tiny office across the hall from the living room, and the doorway after that led to a formal dining room. Tall mahogany cabinets with glass-paned doors lined the walls of the kitchen at the end of the hall. The rooms were small but they held much mystery for Cara and Bobby. The most intriguing room was tucked behind the kitchen at the very back of the house. Mrs. Rodriguez loved to paint and she actually had a painting room. The room was bright and cheerful with a paint-splattered floor and open shelves filled with canvas and brushes. One entire wall was covered with windows, and plants in pots of all shapes and sizes hung in front of the windows.

"This is where I allow myself to make a mess," Mrs. Rodriguez announced. "Maybe one or both of you would like to join me here sometime. Do you like to paint?"

The children's eyes were wide with wonder as they shrugged their shoulders.

Heading upstairs, Mrs. Rodriguez showed them to their rooms. The children were surprised to discover their own clothes hanging in the closets of each of their bedrooms. Cara's only doll lay waiting on her bed, and the shoebox that held Bobby's favorite action figures had been placed on his dresser.

"Andrea, a caseworker from the social service office, brought your things over earlier this afternoon." Mrs. Rodriguez answered their unasked questions.

Two new toothbrushes were still encased in their wrappers and lying on the counter in the bathroom they would share. Mrs. Rodriguez reached into a drawer and grabbed two tubes of toothpaste. "There," she said, putting a tube beside each brush. "You can each have your own tube of toothpaste. This is where we keep the towels and washcloths." She pointed to a closet.

"I want you to make yourselves at home in this house. If you need something you can't find, just ask Mr. Rodriguez or me about it, okay? Now, if you'd like to, you can rest up here for about thirty or forty minutes. After that, I'm going to need you to help me make lemonade. You can come down to the kitchen anytime you want to, or I'll come and get you later. I know it's pretty early in May for a barbeque, but it is a warm day. Mr. Rodriguez is going to fire up the grill, and we'll cook outside. I hope you both like hamburgers."

They nodded silently, and Mrs. Rodriguez left the room.

Bobby and Cara found themselves alone for the first time since they had stepped onto the school bus that morning. They had said very little to any of the strangers they had met today, but now, alone together at last, they were still speechless. So much had happened to them today that they were too overwhelmed to even speak with each other.

Bentley's clicking footsteps on the stairs captured the children's attention, and they walked out into the hallway to greet him. "I'm not tired," Bobby volunteered while scratching Bentley's head.

"Me either," Cara responded.

"Let's go help with the lemonade."

The trio walked to the kitchen together.

"I see rest is the furthest thing from your minds." Mrs. Rodriguez took a bright yellow lemon from the wooden bowl. "I'll slice and you two can take turns squeezing."

Cara and Bobby had never made lemonade with real lemons before. They taste-tested the finished product, and Mrs. Rodriguez continued to add sugar until they all agreed that the lemonade was just right. Mrs. Rodriguez then took a bowl of potato salad from the refrigerator, handed it to Bobby, and asked him to set it on the picnic table. Cara was asked to carry a tray of condiments, and Mrs. Rodriguez followed with the lemonade. The picnic table was already adorned in a red-checked cloth and dark blue dishes. Mr. Rodriguez soon pronounced the burgers ready, and the foster family sat down for their first meal together.

"You know, we have grandchildren just about your ages," Mr. Rodriguez said. "But they live on the other side of the country, and we don't get to see them nearly as often as we would like. We enjoy having kids around, and that's one of the reasons why we're happy that you two are going to be able to spend some time with us."

"I hope you'll think of this as a little vacation," said Mrs. Rodriguez. "Maybe we can come up with some fun activities while you're here."

Cara glanced quickly at the wall of windows separating the painting room from the yard. Mrs. Rodriguez smiled.

"I don't think this is a night for homework, do you?" she asked Mr. Rodriguez. "In fact, I think we should roast marshmallows and then have a painting event."

"What's a painting event?" Bobby asked.

"It's when everyone goes into the painting room, we turn some music on as loud as we want, and we paint one giant picture together. How does that sound?"

"I've never been to a painting event," answered Bobby.

"Me either." Mr. Rodriguez chuckled.

"Do you think you'd enjoy an event like that, Cara?" Mrs. Rodriguez directed her smile at the little girl who sat across the table. Cara nodded her head.

Mr. Rodriguez laughed. "Well then, let the painting event begin."

"Not until after the marshmallows, Miguel." Mrs. Rodriguez smiled. "First thing's first."

After dinner, Mrs. Rodriguez asked the children to help her clear the table while Mr. Rodriguez looked for a few old shirts that soon became their painting smocks. The neighbors probably heard Bon Jovi's voice reverberate across the yard as the artists painted the large canvas. Inspiration sometimes struck them simultaneously, and other times one or more artists stood quietly and admired the work by another. Just before bedtime, they agreed that the work was complete—the most beautiful abstract painting any of them had ever seen.

"Perhaps it will hang in a college museum one day," suggested Mr. Rodriguez.

"You never know, Miguel." Mrs. Rodriguez laughed. She turned to the children. "Time for bed. Cara, I'm going to run your bath water because I want to be certain that it's not too hot for your back. Then I'll give you your privacy, but after you're in your pajamas, I'd like to put medicine on the burns if you'll let me. I'll be very gentle so I don't hurt you, and Bobby can stay with you and hold your hand if you'd like him to do that. How about it? Will you let me do that?"

Cara nodded.

When the children were ready for bed, Mr. and Mrs. Rodriguez said good night and explained that a nightlight would remain on in the hallway so Bobby and Cara could easily find their way around.

"Knock on our bedroom door at any time if you need anything," Mrs. Rodriguez reminded them. "Tomorrow morning Mr. Rodriguez is going to make pancakes. Do you like pancakes?"

"I love them," Cara replied softly.

"Me too," Bobby said. Everyone said a last good night. Fresh sheets crinkled as the children climbed into their beds.

Adrenaline had masked the exhaustion that had built throughout the day, but both Bobby and Cara realized now how tired they were. But they had trouble falling asleep in this strange place. Their minds raced, revisiting the various scenes from the past twenty-four hours. They wondered what might happen tomorrow. Would their father call in the morning?

DIFFERENT TYPES OF FOSTER CARE

The names for various types of foster care can differ from one locale to the next. Basically, however, foster homes can be licensed to provide several types of care.

Short-Term Emergency Care

This is provided to children who need to move out of their home quickly and with little advance notice to the social service agency. Placement is usually only necessary for a day or two to a few weeks. The home provides a safe and nurturing environment for a child while the social service agency is locating a longer placement option.

If a child has been severely traumatized in the home, he may need to be moved quickly to a short-term foster-care placement.

Regular Foster Care

The majority of foster homes provide longer-term care while reunification efforts with a child's biological parents are being conducted or while an adoptive family is being sought.

Therapeutic Foster Care

Foster parents who offer this type of care undergo more advanced and lengthy training in order to provide for children with certain special needs.

Foster/Adoptive Care

In this case, foster parents are housing and caring for a child they hope to adopt.

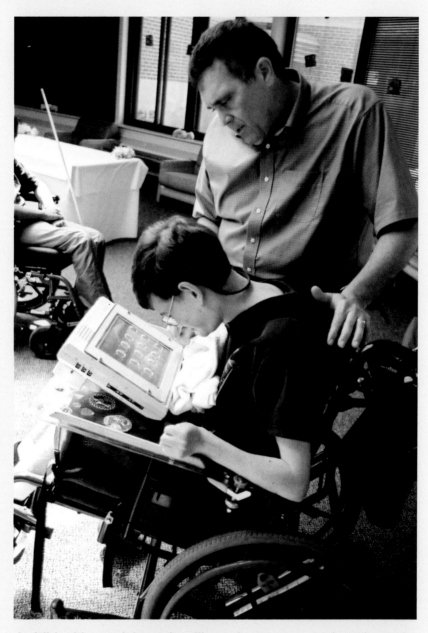

A child with special needs will need extra care and equipment. Foster parents may need additional training.

Respite Foster Care

This version of short-term foster care allows regular or therapeutic foster parents to take a short amount of time away from the foster child in their care.

WHAT DOES "SPECIAL NEEDS" MEAN WHEN IT IS USED TO REFER TO CHILDREN WHO ARE IN FOSTER CARE OR WHO ARE ADOPTED?

Under the Adoption and Safe Families Act, each state is allowed to determine its own definition of children with special needs. Generally, the classification includes those children who have certain physical or behavioral conditions that require continuing medical or therapeutic services. Other conditions that make it more difficult to locate adoptive families for children can be used to determine special needs, including membership in a particular *ethnic* group, having a number of siblings, or being beyond a specified age.

The Adoption and Safe Families Act contains special provisions for adopted children with special needs. These provisions include the following:

- *federal subsidies* for eligible children with special needs
- health insurance (provided by states) for children with special needs who require continuing mental, medical, or rehabilitative care when those children do not qualify for federal subsidies

GROUP HOMES

There are several types of group homes for children needing foster care. Most offer care to older children, usually

The interior of a group home looks very much like any other home.

between the ages of fourteen and eighteen, although some younger children might be accepted. Local governments operate some of these shelters while others are privately owned and operated. Examples of the kinds of care offered at these facilities include the following:

- care and therapy for children with emotional disturbances
- care and therapy for children who exhibit problematic or **delinquent** behavior
- emergency or long-term care for children when home-based foster care is not available
- care and treatment for children with addictions to various substances such as drugs or alcohol

- life training to help older children develop the skills needed to lead a successful life after aging out of the foster-care system (For example, the facility may help children obtain their driver's licenses, learn how to write resumés and conduct themselves in job interviews, balance checkbooks, cook nutritious meals, etc.)

Advantages of Some Group Homes

- trained staff on duty twenty-four hours a day seven days a week
- regular availability of psychologists or social workers for counseling and therapy

Disadvantages of Some Group Homes

- lack of a caring family with good parental role models

ALTERNATIVES TO FOSTER CARE BESIDES ADOPTION

- reunification with biological parents
- emancipation
- guardianship
- kinship care

Reunification

The best-case scenario for foster care is to be able to return the foster child to the care of biological parents. This is possible after the parents have eliminated the problem that made separation from their child necessary. Sometimes children are returned to parents, but a caseworker from social

Kinship care is one foster-care option; a young child such as this one might be placed with an adult brother or sister, or with a grandparent.

services continues to monitor the situation to be certain the child remains properly cared for and safe.

Emancipation

Under certain circumstances, older adolescents can ask the court to change their legal status to that of emancipated youth. This frees the adolescent of the need for foster parents or a guardian. An emancipated youth may have an independent living situation. She could rent her own apartment, for example. An emancipated youth might be eligible to continue receiving support from social services such as having a job coach to assist in locating employment or receiving financial assistance to pay the rent.

Guardianship

A child can be placed under the legal guardianship of an adult that may or may not be related to him. Parents might voluntarily relinquish their parental rights to a grandparent who is willing to accept the responsibility of raising a grandchild, for example.

Kinship Care

In terms of the foster-care system, kinship care is the placing (by social services) of a child into the care of an adult relative rather than into a foster home where the foster parents are not related to the child. This option for foster care has been growing in recent years. In 1996, reports from twenty states indicated that 37 percent of foster children had been placed in kinship care, although the percentage figure varied widely from one state to another. In order to receive payments for foster care, the kinship caregivers must be licensed foster parents. Some states have a more relaxed licensing

process for relatives wishing to offer kinship care than for other prospective foster parents. States are required to consider giving preference to kinship care as opposed to unrelated foster care when placing a child.

THE FIVE STAGES OF GRIEF

In her book, *On Death and Dying*, author and psychiatrist Elisabeth Kübler-Ross describes the five stages of grief that terminally ill people experience. Children and parents who are separated from each other often work through this same series of symptoms leading to acceptance of the situation. The stages are usually, but not always, experienced in the order listed. The stages are:

Stage 1—Denial
Stage 2—Anger

A child who is separated from his parents may need to find appropriate ways to work through his feelings of anger.

Stage 3—Bargaining
Stage 4—Depression
Stage 5—Acceptance/Resolution

These stages often work themselves out in the lives of children and parents in the foster-care system.

Denial

Parents (and children) may initially deny **accusations** and insist that no problem exists. They might try to avoid dealing with the situation. This may be followed by partial acceptance of the situation and denial of the feeling of loss after separation.

Anger

Initial compliance may be followed by confrontational and uncooperative behavior. Both children and parents might become aggressive and demanding.

Bargaining

Anger may be followed by an attempt to negotiate with the individuals in power (caseworkers and foster parents). Compliance with rules may improve.

Depression

Denial, anger, and attempts at deal making may be replaced by a sense of great loss over the reality of the situation. The child might become either very emotional or withdrawn. Parents might perceive the situation as hopeless and begin missing appointments. Both parents and children may feel drained of energy and display a lack initiative.

Research Project

Another book to read about someone who experienced foster care: *The Story of Tracy Beaker* by Jacqueline Wilson. Tracy keeps a funny journal about her experiences in foster home and in a group home.

Acceptance

Over time, most children will develop growing ties to their foster family and begin to identify with them. Emotional distress will decrease with true acceptance of the situation and trust in the foster parents. This final stage might go in two different directions for biological parents. They may acknowledge the fact that certain things have to happen in order for them to be reunited with their children, accept responsibility, and work to make necessary changes in their lives. On the other hand, they may become accustomed to not being with their children and discontinue pursuit of reunification.

Text-Dependent Questions

1. Explain how short-term emergency foster care is different from regular foster care.
2. What are some of the advantages and disadvantages of a group home?
3. What does it mean to be an emancipated youth?
4. What are the five stages that a foster child might go through as she adjusts to being in foster care?

The future is a place of possibility.
—Pearl Crane

Words to Understand

relinquished: Gave up control of something.
custody: Legal control, as of a child by a parent or
other adult.

5

WHAT'S NEXT?

Because of the different time zones and a satellite connection that
kept breaking up, it was very late that evening before Sharon
was finally able to speak with the children's father. Sharon had taken
notes throughout the day, and no detail was spared as she slowly re-
counted the events, including the fact that Mrs. Cooper admitted that
what the children said about her was true. Mrs. Cooper had voluntarily **relinquished** custody of the children late that afternoon. Mr.
Cooper reacted as Sharon expected—with shock followed by denial.

At first, he couldn't imagine his wife hurting Cara like that, but
then he remembered the incident with the head lice that had taken
place the previous year. "So this kind of thing has been going on
whenever I've been away from home?" Mr. Cooper wondered aloud.

Anguish and anger began a vicious tug of war on his emotions as
he silently berated himself for not keeping his children safe. "I don't
even know what to say. Of course I'll telephone the kids in the
morning. It'll be a week or two before I can get there, but then
what?"

He felt out of control, and he hated that feeling. He didn't like
the idea that the state now had **custody** of his children; he didn't like
that at all.

"I know from speaking with your wife that there aren't any
adults in the family who are able to care for the children," Sharon
responded. "As I understand it, your mother is your only living relative, and she's in a nursing home. Your wife's parents are alive, but

her father is an alcoholic who abused both his wife and his daughter when she was growing up. Neither of you has any siblings. That being the situation, the children will definitely have to remain in foster care while you and the caseworker assigned to you and the children work out a plan for their future."

"What kind of a plan are you talking about?"

"The health and safety of your children are our most important concern, Mr. Cooper. Bearing that in mind, we want to do everything possible to assist you in creating a safe environment for them. Andrea—that's your caseworker—will want to meet with you as soon as you arrive in town to discuss the ways we can all work together to accomplish that."

With a sigh, Mr. Cooper agreed.

Bobby opened his eyes in the dimly lit room. His door was open, and the smell of blueberry pancakes was drifting up the stairs. *Mr. Rodriguez sure knows how to cook*, Bobby thought while brushing his teeth and dressing. When he had finished, he pounded on Cara's bedroom door.

Ten minutes later, both children walked through the kitchen door.

"Good morning," Mr. Rodriguez greeted them. "I hope you're hungry. I've been frying pancakes like there's no tomorrow. It's a good thing you got here when you did, though. Mrs. Rodriguez has a big appetite this morning. I wouldn't let her have any of the pancakes until you got here because I was afraid she would eat everything in sight."

"Miguel, you stop filling the kids' heads with nonsense." Mrs. Rodriguez laughed.

The telephone rang just as the delicious meal came to an end.

"Maybe that's our dad," Bobby said.

Mr. Rodriguez answered the phone. He nodded at Bobby and handed him the phone.

"When are you coming to get us?" Bobby asked. He was silent, listening to his father's response.

"No. They're real nice. But we miss you. They have a dog named Bentley." His father said something in his ear and asked a question.

"She's fine." This time Bobby listened for a long time while his father talked.

"Okay. 'Bye."

Bobby handed the phone to Cara. "He wants to talk to you."

"Hi, Daddy. When are you coming to get us?" Cara asked. "Are you bringing Momma with you when you come here? Where is she?"

Once again the children's father spoke for a long time while Cara listened silently. "Okay," she said at last. "'Bye."

Cara held the receiver out to Mr. Rodriguez. "He wants to talk to you again."

"Yes, of course," Mr. Rodriguez said into the phone. "Call as often as you like. I know the children are happy to be able to speak with you, and I know that they're anxious to see you. Just fill us in on what you and Andrea decide concerning the time, and we'll be happy to take the children there."

Mr. Rodriguez turned to the children. "Well, kids, you're going to be able to see your dad in two weeks."

The next two weeks until their father's visit flew by because Mr. and Mrs. Rodriguez knew how to make children feel comfortable and happy. Each night Mrs. Rodriguez knit while sitting in a tall-backed chair in the living room. She'd glance up periodically at Mr. Rodriguez who sat in the middle of the velvet sofa. Bobby was perched on one side of him and Cara sat on the other so that they could each look at *The Secret Garden* as Mr. Rodriguez read the book aloud.

Mrs. Rodriguez dropped off the children and picked them up at school each day, just as she had promised. No one asked Cara or Bobby about Cara's back or anything else when the children returned to school. Bobby did well in school this year, but school was still a constant struggle for Cara.

Cara and Bobby dressed in their favorite clothes on the morning of their first visit with their dad. Mr. and Mrs. Rodriguez were nicely dressed too, as the four of them drove to the social service office.

Mr. Cooper had already spent a considerable amount of time discussing the laws that concern child welfare with Andrea before he arrived in town. Now he was more than ready to see his children.

"Daddy!" Bobby and Cara raced across the visiting room into their father's outstretched arms. He scooped up Cara into the air and let her ride on his shoulders with her arms linked around his neck as Bobby hugged his leg. With one arm supporting Cara, Mr. Cooper ruffled Bobby's hair with his free hand before placing that arm around Bobby's shoulders. Then he let go of the children and greeted Mr. and Mrs. Rodriguez with handshakes as Andrea made the introductions.

"My wife and I are going to do some shopping while you visit the children," Mr. Rodriguez said. "What time would you like us to return, Andrea?"

"I think we need about two hours, Miguel. Do you have your cell phone with you? Can I call you if anything changes?"

The adults agreed to meet later, and then the Rodriguezes left.

Before Mr. Cooper returned to town, Andrea had explained the need to develop a plan for permanency for the children. Mr. Cooper had spent much of the previous two weeks figuring out how he would be able to care for his children. Andrea was developing her own plan for their care, which would go into effect if Mr. Cooper's plan did not work out. Now, Mr. Cooper told Cara and Bobby that he had decided to change jobs and move back to town.

The children shouted in unison and hugged their dad.

"But," Mr. Cooper cautioned, "it's going to take several months for me to make all the arrangements. So the two of you are going to have to remain in foster care during that time. I need for you to be brave and patient."

"Can we stay with Mr. and Mrs. Rodriguez?" Bobby asked. "They're really nice and we like them."

"You and Cara can stay with them for another week, Bobby," Andrea answered. "That will take you through the end of the school year. Mr. and Mrs. Rodriguez only offer emergency foster care. You need a foster family that can house you for a longer period of time. A nice family that is anxious to meet you and really wants the two of you to spend the next few months with them."

Cara and Bobby wondered what the new family would be like. Worry lurked at the backs of their minds during the remainder of the visit with their dad.

UNDER WHAT CIRCUMSTANCES CAN A COURT TERMINATE THE PARENTAL RIGHTS OF BIOLOGICAL PARENTS?

According to the Adoption and Safe Families Act, a court can terminate parental rights if it finds that it is in the best interest of the child to do so because the parents have subjected the child to "aggravated circumstances." Judges are allowed to use their discretion when determining whether particular situations constitute aggravated circumstances, but the federal law provides examples for states to consider when defining these circumstances. Examples listed in the law include: chronic abuse, sexual abuse, torture, and abandonment. The goal is to protect children by ensuring their health and safety.

In most cases, states are required to initiate proceedings to terminate parental rights for abandoned infants, for children who have been in foster care for fifteen of the last twenty-two months, and in any case where a parent has been found guilty of committing a felony assault against the child in question or a sibling of that child.

Although states may differ in what they believe constitutes "aggravated circumstances," the following items are examples of some of the reasons that are typically listed:

- An established history of abuse or neglect exists, there has been little or no demonstrated improvement in the parent's ability to care for the child, and the probability exists that abuse or neglect of the child will reoccur if the child is returned to the parent's care.
- The parent abandoned the child for an established period of time.
- The parent is unable to provide a safe home for the child, and there is a probability that he or she will

continue to be unable to provide a safe home because of substance abuse.

- A year has passed since a child was placed in foster care, and the parent has not made reasonable progress toward correcting the conditions that necessitated removal of the child.

GOING TO COURT

According to the Adoption and Safe Families Act, various administrative and court proceedings and hearings for children in foster care must take place according to an established timetable. For example, the "permanency hearing" must be held within twelve months of placement in foster care.

When a biological parent's rights have been terminated, the permanency hearing must take place even sooner. Foster parents and other caretakers must be given notice of hearings and case reviews and can present information in these proceedings.

Children do not have to be present at many hearings, but other times they do have to testify in criminal or civil cases. It is not always allowable for a foster parent to be present during a child's testimony. In a criminal case, someone has been accused of a crime and is on trial to determine guilt or innocence. In a civil neglect case, evidence is presented regarding removal of the child from the home.

At the hearing, the family court judge will hear evidence regarding the parent's treatment of the child.

The judge's job is to determine what is the best situation for each child.

A defense attorney represents the defendant's legal rights.

PEOPLE INVOLVED IN COURT PROCEEDINGS
Judge

The judge is in charge in the proceedings in a courtroom. When a jury is not necessary to the proceedings, the judge is the person who determines the outcome.

Attorneys

This is another word for lawyer. Three types of lawyers might be present at court hearings involving child custody and foster care:

- The prosecuting attorney is in charge of presenting the case against the defendant.
- The guardian ad litem is the attorney who has been appointed for the child. It is the guardian ad litem's job to make sure that the child's rights are protected.
- The attorney for the defense is there to protect the rights of the defendant.

Court Appointed Special Advocates (CASAs)

These volunteers are not always present because there are not enough volunteers for all the children who could benefit from their services. They help assure that the child's best interests are paramount in the proceedings.

Bailiff

It is this person's job to maintain order. The bailiff might be dressed in a police uniform or may be wearing civilian clothes.

The court clerk records what is said at a hearing.

Research Project

Read *The Pinballs* by Betsy Byars to learn about three children who have been bounced from foster home to home—and how they decided to take control of their lives.

Make Connections

 To help eliminate fear and increase children's comfort levels when they have to appear in court, it's a good idea to visit the courtroom in advance of the trial date so they become familiar with the setting and people. Contact the courthouse by telephone first to schedule a visit and determine whether or not you will have to be accompanied by the caseworker or another individual. If possible, allow the child to sit in the witness chair and practice speaking into the microphone.

Court Reporter

This individual keeps a record of everything that is said in the courtroom during the proceedings.

Court Clerk

This court employee keeps a record for the court.

Text-Dependent Questions

1. List examples of "aggravated circumstances" that might lead to a child being placed in foster care.
2. What do CASAs do for foster children? Are they paid for what they do?

We cannot predict what uncertainties the future holds. We must have a safety net ready for our children.
—Edna Mitchell

Words to Understand

permanent placement: A final home or adult supervision that will not be altered.
foster drift: Being placed in several different foster homes over a number of years.

6

THE WAITING GAME

Andrea believed Mr. Cooper had every intention of moving to town in order to care for Cara and Bobby. She had worked with many families that overcame hardships in order to be reunited with their children. Recently, the court had returned custody of three siblings to a mother who had successfully conquered drug addiction, passed a high school equivalency exam, gotten a driver's license, and found her first job. Nevertheless, according to the laws governing child welfare, Andrea needed to develop an alternate plan to be certain the children would be on a good schedule toward **permanent placement** if Mr. Cooper did not follow through with his promises. She explained to Mr. Cooper that the goal of such concurrent planning is to eliminate **foster drift** in the child welfare system.

A week after visiting with their dad, Bobby and Cara found themselves traveling to a new foster home. Since they didn't own any suitcases, Bobby and Cara placed their belongings in a trash bag, and Mr. Rodriguez loaded the bags into the trunk of Andrea's car. Mr. and Mrs. Rodriguez were used to giving love and attention to foster children and then parting with them, but Cara and Bobby were not accustomed to such partings, and fear of their unknown future made it even more difficult.

"Mr. and Mrs. Peterson have one child, a daughter," Andrea explained while driving them to the opposite side of town. "I think she's a year ahead of you in school, Cara."

Peterson. Cara rolled the name over in her mind without speaking. It sounded familiar to her.

Realizing that the children would probably be with this family for several months, Andrea had worked to place them within their old school district. That's why the name sounded familiar to Cara—the Petersons' daughter had been in Cara's class during her first year of kindergarten.

"I remember you," Holly Peterson announced when Andrea introduced Bobby and Cara. "You were in my kindergarten class, but you were held back."

"Holly, don't be impolite," her mother cautioned while Mr. Peterson carried the trash bags into the small white bungalow.

"I don't want to share my room with her," Holly whispered.

"Don't be mean, Holly," her mother responded quietly, but Cara heard everything she said. "It's not going to be forever, and I want you to be nice to both Cara and Bobby while they're here. Anyway, this is only a three-bedroom house, so you don't have a choice. You have to share your room with Cara." Mrs. Peterson followed her husband into the house.

"I don't like you," Holly whispered in Cara's ear.

Bobby overheard the remark. "Well, we don't like you either." He turned to his sister. "Don't feel bad, Cara. We're not going to be here that long."

But Bobby was wrong. Weeks stretched to months, and months piled upon each other while the children waited for their father.

"I hate your hair," Holly said to Cara on the first day of the new school year.

"Holly!" Mrs. Peterson exclaimed. "How many times do I have to tell you to leave Cara alone?"

Cara didn't respond, and for once, she didn't even blame Holly for the nasty comment. She hated her hair too. Her mother had cropped it off just below ear level after she had head lice, and everyone had been trimming it to that length ever since.

Soon she had more things to add to her list of things she didn't like about herself. After arriving at the Petersons' she had begun to gain weight. Mr. and Mrs. Peterson were nice, but Holly was a different story. She was usually sickeningly sweet in front of her parents, but if their backs were turned, Holly never missed an opportunity to say something mean to Cara. Cara didn't usually respond to Holly's remarks. Instead, Cara sought comfort in Mrs. Peterson's delicious baked goods.

Mrs. Peterson thought both of the children were too thin when they arrived, so she encouraged them to eat her cookies, pies, and cakes. The extra calories Bobby consumed only seemed to make him grow taller, not fatter. Cara had also gotten a little taller over the summer, but she'd gained a significant amount of weight too, and her clothes from the previous school year were now uncomfortably tight.

By October, Bobby was clearly doing well in school, while Cara continued to struggle. She couldn't understand how reading came so easily to other kids. Dread seeped through every pore of her body when she was called upon to read out loud. Her face would turn red as she struggled to sound out words while her classmates listened impatiently.

Halloween found them still with the Petersons, as did Thanksgiving and Christmas. Finally, over the Christmas holiday, they were allowed to have their first overnight visit with their dad in the new apartment he had rented for the three of them. All the furniture from the previous house had been sold because their father didn't want anything that might hold bad memories for Cara or Bobby. As he gave them a tour of their new rooms, Cara admired her new blue and white bedroom. Bobby liked the fact that he had bunk beds. He couldn't wait to invite a friend over.

"When can we move in?"

"Soon, Bobby," his father said. "I still have to make one last trip with the Navy, but then I'll be moving here for good, and the three of us will be a family again."

"What about Momma?" Cara asked.

He and their mother were in the process of getting a divorce, their father explained. Their mother would not be living with them. Cara and Bobby felt sad and strange—but they were also relieved. They each gave a deep sigh, as though a heavy weight they had been carrying all their lives was finally being lifted from their shoulders.

A snowstorm was brewing as the children returned to the Petersons'. They were unhappy to be saying good-bye to their father again, but they were comforted by the knowledge that they'd soon be together for good.

Ice began to quickly build on the Interstate as Mr. Cooper headed toward the airport. As he steered the car carefully, he was glad this would be his last trip away from home. He had noticed Cara's weight gain, and he knew it was a symptom of the stress she had been under for the past several months. He and the children needed to be together.

Then, as he rounded a sharp curve, his heart leapt with fear. Headlights glared in his eyes, headlights headed straight at him. He slammed on his brakes, but his wheels had no traction on the icy road. He smashed into the other car. A few seconds later, the tractor trailer behind him slammed into him from the rear.

Mr. Cooper would never see his children again.

COURT APPOINTED SPECIAL ADVOCATES (CASAS)

In 1977, a judge from Seattle trained volunteers speak in court on behalf of children in foster care. Following on the heels of his success with the program, other judges began to do the same thing. Passage of the Child Abuse Act in 1990 encouraged the expansion of this program. Today there are more than fifty thousand CASA volunteers and more than one million children have received help through this program.

The CASA program is endorsed by the National Council of Juvenile and Family Court Judges, the American Bar Association, the Office of Juvenile Justice and Delinquency Prevention, and the United States Advisory Board on Child Abuse and Neglect.

A lawyer presents information provided by a CASA, a trained volunteer who represents the legal rights of children in foster care.

CASA volunteers do their best to represent the best interests of each child.

CASA volunteers monitor situations, review paperwork, conduct interviews, do research, write reports, and make recommendations concerning the best interests of a child.

Anyone who has good verbal and written communications skills and who can make a time commitment (usually a year, sometimes longer) can volunteer for the CASA program, including college students, as well as people with full-time jobs and those who are retired. Training in specific areas such as interviewing techniques, child development, how various hearings are conducted, and numerous additional topics are provided by CASA programs.

FOSTER CARE IN CANADA

Foster care in Canada falls under the Child, Family, and Community Services Act.

Details regarding foster care programs and the names of various offices differ somewhat from one province to another, but the basic policies and services remain the same.

In Ontario, the Ministry of Community and Social Services develops foster-care policy and reviews programs. There are fifty-four Children's Aid Societies (CAS) that administer foster-care programs in Ontario. They recruit and approve foster parents and manage care.

As in the United States, private organizations and individuals can also be licensed (by the Ministry of Community and Social Services) to administer foster care programs. They cannot place a child in foster care, however; that can only be done by a CAS.

Caseworkers must visit foster-care homes within seven days of having placed foster children there. They must return for a second visit within thirty days and again every three months.

Inquiries by foster parents must be addressed within twenty-four hours. Allegations against foster parents must

Research Project

 Read *I'll Sing You One-O* by Nan Gregory to learn a different perspective from a foster child: what it's like to be separated from a foster home that is all you have ever known, and sent to live with family members whom you have never met before.

be investigated within five working days, and the outcome of the investigation must be presented to the foster parents within five additional working days.

The Residential Placement Advisory Committee reviews placement objections raised by children over the age of twelve.

Like the United States, Canada also provides residential care through group homes.

Home is the place where you know you are welcome.
—Mary North

7

A New Home

"Your dad's dead," Holly reminded Cara while the two girls prepared a salad for supper. After months of not responding to Holly's verbal attacks, Cara finally snapped.

"Shut up!" Cara's hand still held the knife she had been using to cut a tomato. Mrs. Peterson returned just in time to see Cara shouting, and Mrs. Peterson was frightened when she saw Cara holding a knife. Mrs. Peterson grabbed the knife, ordered Cara to her room, and called Andrea.

"I really think the children need to have a new home. Cara just can't get along with Holly."

Cara heard what Mrs. Peterson said, but Cara was happy to be moving. She didn't care where they went. Anywhere would be better than the Petersons'.

Andrea was surprised to receive Mrs. Peterson's call. Cara had never complained about Holly during Andrea's monthly visits to the Peterson home, and the Petersons had never before complained about Cara. Six months had passed since Mr. Cooper's death, the permanency hearing had already taken place, and Andrea needed to find the children an adoptive home. She believed she had located the perfect family for Bobby and Cara and had planned to introduce the children to the Jensens before a possible move there, but Mrs. Peterson now wanted the children to move immediately. Andrea hoped that now she would be able to speed up the process and get Cara and Bobby placed with the Jensens sooner than she had planned.

Mr. and Mrs. Jensen were looking forward to meeting the children. They hoped that their relationship with Cara and Bobby would lead to adoption as it had with Todd, their first foster child.

"Cara would never have hurt Holly," Bobby said to Andrea as they loaded the children's belongings into Andrea's car.

"I'm sure that's true, Bobby, but as I explained earlier, this move doesn't really have anything to do with the incident between Cara and Holly. I think that both you and Cara are going to really like Mr. and Mrs. Jensen and Todd. They're very eager to meet you, and I think you'll be happy with this move.

It was a long drive to the Jensen home, and on the way Andrea told them about their new family.

"Mrs. Jensen teaches Spanish at the high school, and Mr. Jensen works for a large manufacturing plant in the area. Todd is sixteen now. I used to be his caseworker. He moved in with the Jensens as a foster child when he was twelve, and later they adopted him."

"That's not much older than me," Bobby remarked.

"Yes, he was just a year or so older than you at the time," Andrea agreed.

The Jensens lived in a large, freshly painted, old house. It was the last house on a residential street at the edge of town. On one side of the house, children rode bikes and skateboards up and down the sidewalk while dogs barked and chased after the children. If you walked to the other side of the house, however, you could watch dairy cows grazing in pastures down the road.

Cara looked around her as she got out of the car. "This is like a house between two worlds."

A second car pulled in behind them. A teenager was driving, and as he stepped out of the car Andrea smiled. "I almost didn't recognize you, Todd. You must have grown at least a foot since I last saw you. And I see you already have your driver's license!"

Todd gave Andrea a hug. "It's me all right. I got my driver's license about a month ago. This must be Cara and Bobby. Hi, I'm Todd. Mom sent me to the store to pick up some things for your new bedroom. Actually, she already had Dad and I paint both bedrooms, but she has something special planned for your room, Cara. I'm sure Mom and Dad are in the house; they must not have heard our cars. Follow me. I'll introduce you. Let me help you with your stuff, and I'll come back for the rest of these things later."

Bobby and Cara bent to pet a chubby orange cat as they climbed the back stairs. "Is this your cat?" Cara asked, her voice barely louder than a whisper.

"That's Molly. She's the family cat, so actually, she's also your cat, Cara, and yours too, Bobby," Todd replied.

Inside the kitchen, Mrs. Jensen was cleaning green beans. When Mrs. Jensen smiled and greeted everyone, Cara began to relax. The plump cat and Mrs. Jensen's smile told her that this place would be different from the Petersons'.

Mr. Jensen stepped from the hallway into the kitchen. "This must be Cara and Bobby. We're so happy you're finally here. I just finished putting up new shelving in your bedroom." He smiled at Bobby. "I hope you're going to like it."

"Thanks." So far, Bobby liked everything about this place.

"Let me just finish this last batch of beans," Mrs. Jensen said, "and we'll show you around the house. I hope you're going to like your rooms. Andrea told us what your favorite colors are, and we've been having great fun getting the rooms ready for you. Haven't we, Todd?"

"We sure have." Todd rolled his eyes, and everyone laughed.

WHAT HAPPENS TO CHILDREN WHO TURN EIGHTEEN WHILE IN FOSTER CARE?

Each year between sixteen thousand and twenty thousand young people "age out" of foster care. In the past, many of them left foster care without understanding basic life skills such as how to balance a checkbook or drive a car. Many did not know how to get a job and were not prepared to enter the work force. The result was that a large percentage of young adults coming out of foster care ended up homeless. Today, legislation has been passed that makes it possible to offer better transition services, including more education and life training, to individuals as they age out of the foster-care system.

Teens may also need good foster homes.

If a young adult "ages out" of the foster-care system without a good plan for the future, he may end up homeless.

There were once more African American children in the foster-care system than there are children from any other ethnic group.

MULTIETHNIC PLACEMENT

Children of African descent represent a large number of children in foster care. On average, they spend the longest amount of time waiting for adoption and have the greatest risk of never being adopted.

The U.S. Congress determined that this situation had two main causes:

- Many foster and adoption agencies had racial matching policies because they believed it was in the best interest of children to only be placed with parents of the same race as the child.
- In the past, many foster and adoption agencies had policies that discouraged members of some minorities from volunteering to become foster and adoptive parents.

In an effort to ensure that all children in the foster-care system have the homes they need, the Multiethnic Placement Act encourages foster placement that mixes ethnic groups.

In an effort to correct the situation, Congress passed the Multiethnic Placement Act in 1994 and amended it with the Interethnic Adoption Provisions of 1996.

The Multiethnic Placement Act and the Interethnic Adoption Provisions

Both of these laws remove barriers to interracial and inter-ethnic placement for hundreds of thousands of children. They accomplish this by:

- requiring foster and adoption agencies to actively recruit more ethnically and racially diverse foster and adoptive parents
- making it illegal to delay or deny placement of a child

Research Project

Read *Love, Sara* by Mary Beth Lundgren. It's a series of e-mail exchanges and diary entries that describe a foster child's journey toward being able to trust.

because of the child's or the prospective foster or adoptive parent's race or ethnicity

The Indian Child Welfare Act

Congress has determined that it is in the best interest of American Indian children who are in need of foster care or permanent placement through adoption to, whenever possible, remain in the Indian community. This law establishes that policy. The goal is to protect both the rights of the Indian child and the Indian tribe. The law applies to children who are members of American Indian tribes or who are eligible to become members of American Indian tribes.

Most American Indian tribes operate a social services office at their tribal headquarters and oversee foster care placement of Indian children who are members of that tribe.

Text-Dependent Questions

1. Explain why Congress passed a law that encourages children being placed in foster homes that might not match their ethnic background.
2. What ethnic group does this not apply to?

Family means putting your arms around
each other and being there.
—Barbara Bush

8

STEPPING INTO
TOMORROW

Cara was speechless as she stood at the doorway of her new bedroom. Bright yellow walls made the room look like a summer day, and the green furniture reminded Cara of a park.

"It's pretty," she finally said.

"Look at this." Mrs. Jensen sat on the bed and patted the space beside her. Cara sat down, and Mrs. Jensen showed her a catalog. "I thought you could pick out a few of these stencils. Then we could paint some birds and flowers on the walls. Would you like that?"

Cara nodded.

Bobby was also excited with his blue bedroom. One entire wall was filled with shelves, and a new baseball hat and glove had been placed on one of them.

"Andrea told us that you like baseball. Is that right, Bobby?" Todd asked.

Bobby nodded. "But I haven't had a chance to play it all that much."

"I bet Todd's going to make sure you become an experienced player real soon. He's one of the top players on the high school team." Bobby could hear the pride in Mr. Jensen's voice.

Todd shrugged. "All of us kids in the neighborhood like to play in the field next to the house. Sometimes we even get several parents to join in. I think you and Cara will have fun playing too. Even Mom plays sometimes." Todd laughed. "Would you like to see my room?"

Todd's room was dark purple, and bright posters covered most of the walls.

"Cool," Bobby said.

"Way cool," Cara agreed.

Over the next several months, the family spent many evenings playing ball, but they also spent time in the comfortable family room. A cabinet on one wall housed well-used board games that became better used as family members got to know each other.

Mr. Jensen was great at thinking up adventures. One night he took all his fishing poles out of the garage, and the family hiked up to their neighbors' pond, where they caught enough bluegills for dinner the next evening.

As they sat on the bank watching the sun sink, Cara and Bobby told the Jensens about their father and how sad they were when he died. They still missed their father—but now that they lived with the Jensens, somehow they didn't feel as sad as they had at the Petersons'.

Summer drifted into fall, and the children started attending a new school. The transition went well because they had already made many friends in their new neighborhood. Cara's reading had even improved, because everyone in the family took turns reading with her. She had had lots of practice reading aloud over the summer.

Mr. Jensen orchestrated his biggest adventure for an autumn weekend. The excitement in the house grew as camping equipment was hauled out of storage and new sleeping bags were purchased for Bobby and Cara. The family left their car with a canoeing outfitter who then drove them several miles upstream on a local river. They packed their gear into two canoes, put on their life jackets, and climbed on board, Mrs. Jensen and Todd in one canoe and Mr. Jensen, Bobby, and Cara in the other.

Mr. Jensen paddled at the back of the canoe while Bobby and Cara took turns paddling at the front and resting in the center. Trees covering the riverbanks were alive with orange and red. The family floated down the river, the sun warm on their heads.

"Rapids ahead," Todd yelled.

Everyone became alert, and Cara, who was sitting in the center of the canoe, gripped its sides.

"Don't worry," Mr. Jensen reassured them. "The man at the canoe rental told me about this. Little rapids surround a small island up ahead. It'll be fun going through them, and the river is quiet again on the other side."

"Here we go," Mrs. Jensen called as she and Todd hit the rapids first.

"Yee-hah!" Bobby exclaimed as their canoe followed, and Cara squealed in delight.

Stars filled the sky as the family sat around their campfire later that evening.

"I loved this day." Everyone smiled at Cara's remark.

"You know what I love?" Mr. Jensen asked.

"What?" Cara asked.

"I love all of you."

Mrs. Jensen cleared her throat. "Maybe this is a good time for us to tell Cara and Bobby how happy we've all been since they came to live with us. You two know that we are hoping to adopt you. We don't want to pressure you, but we have been wondering how each of you feels about that."

Bobby looked up at the stars. "It makes me happy," he said.

"Me too," Cara said softly.

Todd smiled at them. "I started feeling like I have a little brother and sister the first day you two arrived."

"All right then." Mr. Jensen looked relieved and happy. "I'm going to telephone Andrea as soon as we get home and tell her that we want to make this official."

They put out the fire and climbed into the tent. Their sleeping bags lay crowded together in the dark. The children felt warm and safe.

"If we're going to be a family, what should we call you?" Bobby whispered into darkness.

"Well," Mr. Jensen answered, "as soon as you're comfortable with it, I hope you'll both call us Mom and Dad."

Cara listened to the soft sounds of breathing all around her. She thought about the houses where they had stayed since they stopped living with their mother. Now at last they had found a home.

She smiled. "Good night, Mom and Dad."

FIRST ADOPTION LAW IN THE UNITED STATES

In the mid-1800s, Massachusetts set the following criteria for legal adoption:

- petition from the parents wishing to adopt
- written consent of the biological parents
- judge's determination that the adoption is proper and fitting
- agreement by the biological parents to completely sever their relationship with the child

ADOPTION 2002 INITIATIVE

Everyone agrees with the goal of reducing the number of children in foster care. Toward that goal, the federal government has paid states for adoptions over the established goals according to the Adoption 2002 Initiative.

A child who finds a permanent home with an adoptive family often has more emotional security than if he were in a foster home.

Bonus Money Paid to States

1998	$20 million
1999	$19.3 million
2000	$11 million
2001	$17.5 million

This bonus money was spent to:

- provide increased training for involved staff.
- provide activities and publicity to promote adoption and recruit prospective families.
- provide necessary legal services to expedite the adoption process.
- provide after-adoption services to children and families.
- provide other adoption-related enhancements and services.

After-adoption services help the new family to grow close.

SHARED FAMILY CARE—AN INNOVATIVE PROGRAM IN FOSTER CARE

Many social service agencies are striving to find better ways to protect and care for children who need services while keeping biological families **intact**. Some of these programs provide early intervention to at-risk families so that problems can be corrected before there is a need to remove children. Aid may be offered to parents in the form of vocational training or treatment for substance abuse. Funds might be provided for food and clothing or transportation or child care. Mental health services may be made available for children or parents.

Among the most innovative are programs that call for the at-risk family (often a single mother and her children) to move into the home of a mentor who is paid by the social service agency to model good parenting. In this Shared Family Care, the at-risk and mentor parents may work out budgets and shop together, plan meals and perhaps cook

Shared family care provides mentors and other support to at-risk families.

Research Project

Read *Returnable Girl* by Pamela Lowell. The author is a social worker who works with foster kids.

together, and have various discussions about how to raise a family while working at a job. This approach has the added benefit of providing twenty-four hour a day supervision of the at-risk parent and children. Although availability of the program is very limited, it is available in ten states.

Only a few studies have been conducted to determine the results of Shared Family Care, but they indicate the following:

- The job rate for parents who completed the program doubled.
- Living conditions for families who completed the program improved.
- The program generally lasted less than twelve months. (The average length of time children spend in traditional foster care is twelve to eighteen months.)
- Compared to children who are reunited with their biological family after traditional foster care, children in this program were twice as likely to avoid reentry into the welfare system.

Text-Dependent Questions

1. How long ago was the first documented adoption?
2. Describe shared family care.

FURTHER READING

Beam, Cris. *To the End of June: The Intimate Life of American Foster Care.* New York, Houghton Mifflin, 2013.

Cameron, Theresa. *Foster Care Odyssey: A Black Girl's Story.* Jackson: University of Mississippi Press, 2007.

Imre Geis, Alissa, Marcia Kahn Wright, and Jennifer Wilgocki. *Maybe Days: A Book for Children in Foster Care.* Washington, D.C.: Magination, 2002.

McLain Paula. *Like Family: Growing Up in Other People's Houses: A Memoir.* New York: Little Brown & Company, 2004.

National Court Appointed Special Advocate Association (ed.). *Lighting the Way: Volunteer Child Advocates Speak Out.* Washington, D.C.: CWLA Press, 2002.

Nelson, Claudia. *Little Strangers: Portrayals of Adoption and Foster Care in America, 1850–1929.* Bloomington: Indiana University Press, 2003.

Temple-Plotz, Lana, Ted P. Strickett, and Michael Sterba. *Practical Tools for Foster Parents.* Boys Town, Neb.: Boys Town Press, 2002.

FOR MORE INFORMATION

All About Emil
Personal site operated by a former social worker offering entertaining
graphics and some good information on court proceedings
emilville.com

Camp To Belong
summer camp reunification for siblings placed in separate foster homes
www.camptobelong.org

Casey Family Programs
services for children and youth
www.casey.org

Child Welfare League of America
www.cwla.org

Foster Parent Community
offers on-line training and guest-speaker chat rooms
www.fosterparents.com

Largest Foster Parenting Site on the Internet
www.fosterparenting.com

National CASA Organization
www.nationalcasa.org

National Foster Care Coalition
nfpaonline.org

Publisher's Note:

The websites listed on these pages were active at the time of publication.
The publisher is not responsible for websites that have changed their
address or discontinued operation since the date of publication. The
publisher will review and update the websites upon each reprint.

SERIES GLOSSARY
OF KEY TERMS

Accessibility: An environment that allows people with disabilities to participate as much as they can.

Accommodation: A change in how a student receives instruction, without substantially changing the instructional content.

Achievement test: A standardized test that measures a student's performance in academic areas such as math, reading, and writing.

Acting out: Behavior that's inappropriate within the setting.

Adaptive behavior: The extent to which an individual is able to adjust to and apply new skills to new environments, tasks, objects, and people.

Ambulatory: Able to walk independently.

American Sign Language (ASL): A language based on gestures that is used by people who are deaf in the United States and Canada.

Americans with Disabilities Act (ADA): In 1990, Congress passed this act, which provides people who have disabilities with the same freedoms as Americans who do not have disabilities. The law addresses access to buildings and programs, as well as housing and employment.

Anxiety: An emotional state of fear, often not attached to any direct threat, which can cause sweating, increased pulse, and breathing difficulty.

Aphasia: Loss of the ability to speak.

Articulation: The ability to express oneself through sounds, words, and sentences.

Asperger syndrome: An disorder that is on the autism spectrum, which can cause problems with nonverbal learning disorder and social interactions.

Assessment: The process of collecting information about a student's learning needs through tests, observations, and interviewing the student, the family, and others. Assistive technology: Any item or piece of equipment that is used to improve the capabilities of a child with a disability.

Attention-deficit/hyperactivity Disorder (ADHD): A disorder that can cause inappropriate behavior, including poor attention skills, impulsivity, and hyperactivity.

Autism spectrum disorder: A range of disabilities that affect verbal and nonverbal communication and social interactions.

122

Bipolar disorder: A brain disorder that causes uncontrollable changes in moods, behaviors, thoughts, and activities.

Blind (legally): Visual acuity for distance vision of 20/200 or less in the better eye after best correction with conventional lenses; or a visual field of no greater than 20 degrees in the better eye.

Bullying: When a child faces threats, intimidation, name-calling, gossip, or physical violence.

Cerebral palsy (CP): Motor impairment caused by brain damage during birth or before birth. It can be mild to severe, does not get worse, and cannot be cured. Chronic: A condition that persists over a long period of time.

Cognitive: Having to do with remembering, reasoning, understanding, and using judgment.

Congenital: Any condition that is present at birth.

Counseling: Advice or help through talking, given by someone qualified to give such help.

Deaf: A hearing loss so severe that speech cannot be understood, even with a hearing aid, even if some sounds may still be perceived.

Developmental: Having to do with the steps or stages in growth and development of a child.

Disability: A limitation that interferes with a person's ability to walk, hear, talk, or learn.

Down syndrome: An abnormal chromosomal condition that changes the development of the body and brain, often causing intellectual disabilities.

Early intervention: Services provided to infants and toddlers ages birth to three who are at risk for or are showing signs of having a slower than usual development.

Emotional disturbance (ED): An educational term (rather than psychological) where a student's inability to build or maintain satisfactory interpersonal relationships with peers and teachers, inappropriate types of behavior or feelings, and moods of unhappiness or depression get in the way of the student being able to learn and function in a school setting.

Epilepsy: A brain disorder where the electrical signals in the brain are disrupted, causing seizures. Seizures can cause brief changes in a person's body movements, awareness, emotions, and senses (such as taste, smell, vision, or hearing).

Fine motor skills: Control of small muscles in the hands and fingers, which are needed for activities such as writing and cutting.

Gross motor skills: Control of large muscles in the arms, legs, and torso, which are needed for activities such as running and walking.

Hard-of-hearing: A hearing loss that may affect the student's educational performance.

Heredity: Traits acquired from parents.

Individualized Education Plan (IEP): A written education plan for students ages 5 to 22 with disabilities, developed by a team of professionals, (teachers, therapists, etc.) and the child's parent(s), which is reviewed and updated yearly. It contains a description of the child's level of development, learning needs, goals and objectives, and services the child will receive.

Individuals with Disabilities Education Act (IDEA): The Individuals with Disabilities Education Act (IDEA) is the nation's federal special education law that requires public schools to serve the educational needs of students with disabilities. IDEA requires that schools provide special education services to eligible students as outlined in a student's IEP, and it also provides very specific requirements to guarantee a free appropriate education for students with disabilities in the least restrictive environment.

Intervention: A planned activity to increase students' skills.

Learning disability: A general term for specific kinds of learning problems that can cause a person to have challenges learning and using certain skills, such as reading, writing, listening, speaking, reasoning, and doing math.

Least restrictive environment: The educational setting or program that provides a student with as much contact as possible with children without disabilities, while still appropriately meeting all of the child's learning and physical needs.

Mainstreaming: Providing any services, including education, for children with disabilities, in a setting with other children who do not have disabilities.

Motor: Having to do with muscular activity.

Nonambulatory: Not able to walk independently.

Occupational therapist (OT): A professional who helps individuals be able to handle meaningful activities of daily life such as self-care skills, education, recreation, work or social interaction.

Palate: The roof of the mouth.

Paraplegia: Paralysis of the legs and lower part of the body.

Partially sighted: A term formally used to indicate visual acuity of 20/70 to 20/200, but also used to describe visual impairment in which usable vision is present.

Pediatrics: The medical treatment of children.

Physical therapist (PT): A person who helps individuals improve the use of bones, muscles, joints, and/or nerves.

Prenatal: Existing or occurring prior to birth.

Quadriplegia: Paralysis affecting all four limbs.

Referral: In special education, students are referred for screening and evaluation to see if they are eligible for special education services.

Self-care skills: The ability to care for oneself; usually refers to basic habits of dressing, eating, etc.

Special Education: Specialized instruction made to fit the unique learning strengths and needs of each student with disabilities in the least restrictive environment.

Speech impaired: Communication disorder such as stuttering, impaired articulation, a language impairment, or a voice impairment, which adversely affects a child's educational performance.

Speech pathologist: A trained therapist, who provides treatment to help a person develop or improve articulation, communication skills, and oral-motor skills.

Spina bifida: A problem that happens in the first month of pregnancy when the spinal column doesn't close completely.

Standardized tests: Tests that use consistent directions, procedures, and criteria for scoring, which are often administered to many students in many schools across the country.

Stereotyping: A generalization in which individuals are falsely assigned traits they do not possess based on race, ethnicity, religion, disability, or gender.

Symptom: An observable sign of an illness or disorder.

Syndrome: A set of symptoms that occur together.

Therapy: The treatment or application of different techniques to improve specific conditions for curing or helping to live with various disorders.

Traumatic Brain Injury (TBI): Physical damage to the brain that could result in physical, behavioral, or mental changes depending on which area of the brain is injured.

Visually impaired: Any degree of vision loss that affects an individual's ability to perform the tasks of daily life, which is caused by a visual system that is not working properly or not formed correctly.

Vocational education: Educational programs that prepare students for paid or unpaid employment, or which provide additional preparation for a career that doesn't require a college degree.

INDEX

ABOUT THE AUTHOR
AND THE CONSULTANTS

Joyce Libal is a writer and artist living with her husband and assorted pets on their orchard in the mountains of northeastern Pennsylvania. When she is not writing, Joyce enjoys painting, quilting, and gardening. She has written several books for other Mason Crest series, including NORTH AMERICAN FOLKLORE and PSYCHIATRIC DISORDERS: DRUGS AND PSYCHOLOGY FOR THE MIND AND BODY.

Dr. Lisa Albers is a developmental behavioral pediatrician at Children's Hospital Boston and Harvard Medical School, where her responsibilities include outpatient pediatric teaching and patient care in the Developmental Medicine Center. She currently is Director of the Adoption Program, Director of Fellowships in Developmental and Behavioral Pediatrics, and collaborates in a consultation program for community health centers. She is also the school consultant for the Walker School, a residential school for children in the state foster care system.

Dr. Carolyn Bridgemohan is an instructor in pediatrics at Harvard Medical School and is a board-certified developmental behavioral pediatrician on staff in the Developmental Medicine Center at Children's Hospital, Boston. Her clinical practice includes children and youth with autism, hearing impairment, developmental language disorders, global delays, mental retardation, and attention and learning disorders. Dr. Bridgemohan is coeditor of *Bright Futures Case Studies for Primary Care Clinicians: Child Development and Behavior*, a curriculum used nationwide in pediatric residency training programs.

Cindy Croft is the State Special Needs Director in Minnesota, coordinating Project EXCEPTIONAL MN, through Concordia University. Project EXCEPTIONAL MN is a state project that supports the inclusion of children in community settings through training, on-site consultation, and professional development. She also teaches as adjunct faculty for Concordia University, St. Paul, Minnesota. She has worked in the special needs arena for the past fifteen years.

Dr. Laurie Glader is a developmental pediatrician at Children's Hospital in Boston where she directs the Cerebral Palsy Program and is a staff pediatrician with the Coordinated Care Services, a program designed to meet the needs of children with special health care needs. Dr. Glader also teaches regularly at Harvard Medical School. Her work with public agencies includes New England SERVE, an organization that builds connections between state health departments, health care organizations, community providers, and families. She is also the staff physician at the Cotting School, a school specializing in the education of children with a wide range of special health care needs.